THE CHAPEL OF PRINCETON UNIVERSITY

THE CHAPEL
OF PRINCETON
UNIVERSITY
By Richard Stillwell

PRINCETON UNIVERSITY PRESS

PRINCETON, NEW JERSEY 1971

Frontispiece: Quatrefoil
from Tympanum of Southeast Porch,
Symbolic Flowers and Plants

Copyright © 1971
by Princeton University Press
ALL RIGHTS RESERVED
L. C. Card 76-90961
I.S.B.N. 0-691-03864-3

Publication of this book has been aided
by the Friends of the Chapel

This book is composed in Linotype Baskerville

Printed in the United States of America
by the Meriden Gravure Company,
Meriden, Connecticut

TO ALL THE ARTISTS
TO WHOSE SKILL AND UNDERSTANDING
THIS CHAPEL IS A PERPETUAL TESTIMONY
TO ALL THEIR HELPERS, ARTISANS AND TECHNICIANS
WITHOUT WHOSE LOYAL COOPERATION
THE WORK COULD NOT HAVE BEEN ACCOMPLISHED
AND ABOVE ALL TO
JOHN GRIER HIBBEN, PRESIDENT OF PRINCETON UNIVERSITY
AND TO ALBERT MATHIAS FRIEND, JR.
TO WHOSE PATIENT AND UNTIRING DIRECTION
THE PROGRAM AND ICONOLOGY OF THE SCULPTURE
AND OF THE STAINED GLASS ARE DUE
AND TO THE MANY DONORS
WHOSE NAMES ARE RECORDED ELSEWHERE
THIS BOOK IS DEDICATED
IN GRATEFUL ADMIRATION
AND AFFECTION

*"By Their Works Ye Shall
Know Them"*

PREFACE

THE purpose of this book is to give the visitor as complete a description of the Chapel as possible so that, provided he has the patience to follow the symbolism of the carving and the stained-glass windows, he will come to realize that the decoration of the building contains the essence of the Old and the New Testaments, both of which appear on the seal of Princeton University. He will also become conscious of the immense amount of thought and skill that has been expended on the monument.

In compiling the book I have worked through all the records available to me and have quoted extensively from the booklet entitled "The University Chapel" (5th ed., 1954). Much of the material consulted is in the form of notes by Professor A. M. Friend, who was in charge of organizing and planning the iconography of the sculpture and the windows. His correspondence with the architect, Ralph Adams Cram, and with the sculptors and glass-makers has been especially helpful. While the building was under construction, I was fortunate to have had frequent access to it and to have enjoyed many instructive conversations with Professor Friend, both then and later. Miss Rosalie Green, Director of the Index of Christian Art, has given me valuable information and I am indebted to Professor Henry L. Savage, who obtained from Professor Mario Nati, Deputy Director of the "Istituto Italiano di Cultura," the interpretation of a detail in one of the choir windows. The Reverend Frederic E. Fox, Recording Secretary of the University, has provided the lists of memorials and donors which appear as an Appendix. From the Friends of the Chapel and especially from Mrs. Barton Thomas the book has received continuing support.

Finally, I would express my gratitude to Ernest Gordon, Dean of the Chapel, for his interest, and his unfailing help and encouragement in this work.

November 1, 1970   Richard Stillwell

Acknowledgment for photographs is made to the following:
Charles J. Connick Associates: Plates 11–21
Ira W. Martin: color plate of the Great West Window
Elizabeth Menzies: Plates 1, 3–10
Princeton University Archives: Plate 2

The artist's sketch which is used as frontispiece
was kindly supplied by Lydia Tabor Poe.

CONTENTS

* The numbers in parentheses refer to the numbering of the
windows as shown on the Plan of the Chapel on page 6.

LIST OF ILLUSTRATIONS

COLOR PLATES

TEXT FIGURES

GLOSSARY

apsidal	having a semicircular plan
boss	ornamental carving at the intersection of the ribs of a vault
buttress	short section of heavy wall, usually at right angles to the side wall, that serve to steady it and also absorb the thrust of the vaults
clerestory	the level of the windows that give light to the upper part of the nave
colonnette	small column or shaft generally attached to the pier or wall
corbel	bracket
formeret	shaft that defines the angle where the severies of a vault come against the wall
ground story arcade	the main series of arches flanking the nave at ground level
hood-mold	molding over the heads of windows, frequently extending part way down the sides
lancet	vertical panel of a window, usually terminating in an ornamental tracery
lozenge	diamond-shaped panel
mandorla	an almond-shaped surround to a figure, signifying glory. Usually found with depictions of Christ

narthex	the vestibule of a church
paten	a flat dish or plate, associated with the service of Holy Communion
pier	vertical support, generally made up of moldings or colonnettes that serve to support arches or lintels
predella	a panel below a principal figure of scene
rebus	punning device, such as a pine-cone for Pyne. Often used in heraldry
rib	the molded element that separates the sections of the vaulting
severy	the area, generally triangular, that fills the space between the ribs
string-course	a continuous molding that divides a wall into horizontal zones
tierceron	rib between the diagonal ribs that subdivide a vault
trefoil	literally, a three-leaf pattern
triforium	a gallery immediately above the main arcade, generally opposite the level of the roof over the side aisles
tunnel vault	a vault that rests for its entire length on the walls below, as in a tunnel
tympanum	the panel above the horizontal lintel of a doorway. It may be semicircular or pointed according to the style
vaulting shaft	shaft (colonnette) forming part of a pier, and carried up to the springing of the vault ribs.

THE CHAPEL OF PRINCETON UNIVERSITY

THE PRESENT CHAPEL
AND ITS
PREDECESSORS

FOR almost a century the chapel of the College of New Jersey was located in what ultimately became the Faculty Room, in the south wing of Nassau Hall. This "Old Prayer Hall" was replaced in 1847 by a chapel erected a short distance east of Nassau Hall on a site later occupied by a portion of the Pyne Library. The cruciform plan and the introduction of an organ occasioned some concern on the part of the Trustees, who regarded the one as a reflection of popery and the other as an instrument too worldly for the strict Presbyterian traditions of the College.

Following the Civil War the undergraduate body doubled in size, and in 1881 adequate and dignified accommodations for worship were provided by a munificent gift from Henry G. Marquand. The old chapel became a lecture and recitation hall until it was demolished in 1897 to make way for the Pyne Library.

The Marquand Chapel, as it was known, stood a little south of the western end of the present Chapel, and was designed by Richard Morris Hunt in the Romanesque style then popular in this country. The building was cruciform in plan with wooden vaulting over the central portion and a masonry half-dome over the eastern end, where the arrangement conformed to the usual type associated with the Presbyterian church.

During house-party weekend in the spring of 1920, one of Princeton's more spectacular fires spread from an old recitation building, Dickinson

Facing page:
1 West portal

4

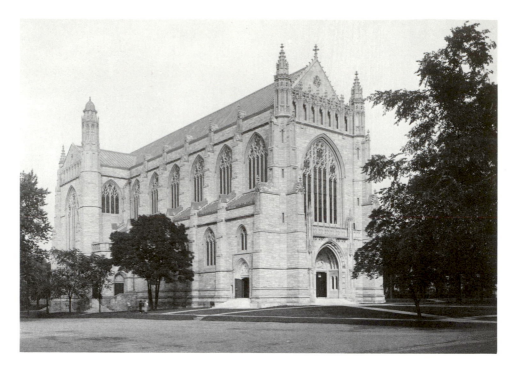

2 The Chapel from the Northwest

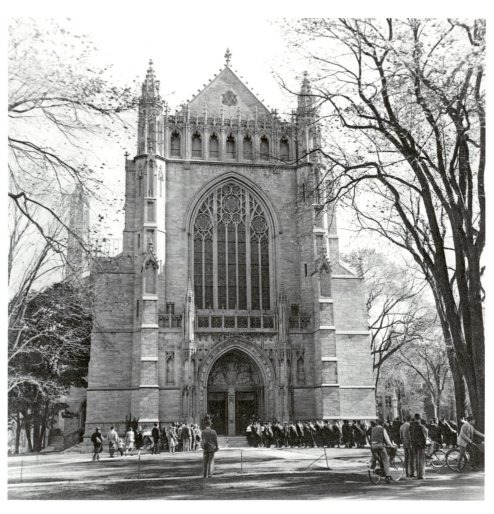

3 West Facade

Hall, and, fanned by a strong north wind, threatened the Joseph Henry House. This house then stood immediately to the south of Dickinson Hall, while the Marquand Chapel, still farther south, was, because of its stone walls and heavy slate roof, considered immune. Valiant efforts by the fire department kept the house well wetted down, but sparks were carried into the small ventilating louvres in the chapel roof and soon ignited the timbering between the roof and the wooden ceiling. By the time this was observed, the chapel was hopelessly aflame and was totally destroyed.

THE DESIGN OF THE CHAPEL

PLANS were shortly made for the construction of the new chapel, and in the interval between its completion and the destruction of its predecessor services were held in Alexander Hall. The cornerstone was laid in 1925 and the Chapel dedicated in 1928. There could be little question as to the general style of the new building. Since the construction of the Pyne Library in 1896, Princeton had been committed to the Collegiate Gothic, and several dormitories, as well as the gymnasium and McCosh Hall, had already been built.

One of the leading Gothicists in the country at that time was Ralph Adams Cram, supervising architect of the University and architect of several of its buildings, including the Graduate College, finished less than ten years before.

The architect's approach to the design is characteristically embodied in a conversation held during the summer of 1929 between him and a Princeton Alumnus, T. H. Vail Motter. It is also reflected in an article which Cram wrote in May 1928 for the *Princeton Alumni Weekly*. Here he dwells on the evocative and constructive power of architecture as a living and creative force, "a center of dynamic energy." In reply to the question: "Is Gothic connected with our time?," Cram answered that he regarded contemporary use of it as a renascence not of pagan but of Christian forms. According to him the drawing power of architecture guarantees accessions through the years. The windows remaining to be filled, he said, "will come easily" and he looked forward to that "unending process that will give a certain life, through progressive growth to what would otherwise be but an architectural essay, static, material, without the informing breath of life."

It is significant that the prophecy of the architect has come true. Within forty years all the remaining windows of the Chapel have been filled and the building has become increasingly a focus of spiritual life on the campus.

The design of the Chapel is one for which no exact historical precedent can be found. The usual type of college chapel is to be seen in the chapels of Oxford and Cambridge. These structures, perfect in their way, were designed for a relatively small number of students, all of whom were to be

E

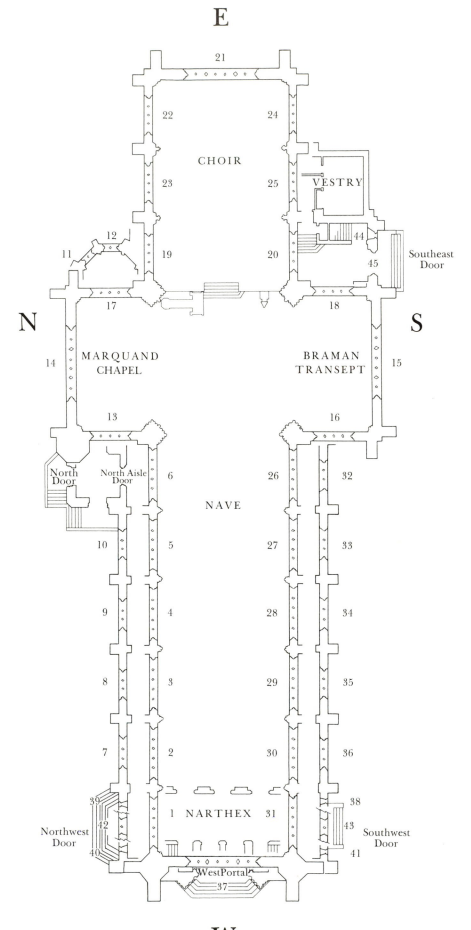

N

S

21

22   24

CHOIR

23   25   VESTRY

12   44

11   19   20   45   Southeast
Door

17   18

MARQUAND   BRAMAN
CHAPEL   TRANSEPT

14   15

13   16

North
Door   North Aisle
Door   6   26   32

NAVE

10   5   27   33

9   4   28   34

8   3   29   35

7   2   30   36

39   38

1   NARTHEX   31

Northwest   42   43   Southwest
Door   Door

40   41

WestPortal

37

Plan of the Chapel

W

seated in a chancel or choir, which formed the major part of the building. Such space as was provided for the public consisted of a small and unimportant ante-chapel. The only exception is the great chapel of King's College, Cambridge, and the exception is apparent rather than real in that the choir at King's is separated by a screen from the nave, which is therefore of very little practical importance for the routine services of a small college body.

The typical English collegiate arrangement was thus out of the question here. The general plan of the Princeton Chapel does not differ much from the large parish church or small cathedral typical of the Middle Ages. It consists of a nave of six bays, crossing, transepts, and choir. It recalls the English chapel or abbey tradition in that the choir is unusually large and without aisles. However, any English church of the same size would be certain to have a tower at the west end, or the crossing, or both. Here, as at King's, the roof runs in an unbroken line from end to end. Another differ- *Plate 3* ence is that in a mediaeval building the architectural aisles would be much wider than at Princeton, where they are used not for seating but merely for passage. *Plate 4*

The factor that determines the general line of the entire building is the presence and use of a masonry-vaulted ceiling. The interior shows the three stories typical of such a vaulted structure—ground story arcade, triforium or arcaded gallery opening into the space covered by the aisle roof, and clerestory. The general proportions—especially the low triforium— *Plate 6* are like many English churches, but the vault itself and its supporting colonnettes are developed after the manner of the perfected French vaults.

Over each bay of nave and choir the transverse and diagonal ribs define four triangular severies or panels, each of which, from below, is slightly concave. Thus the filling is supported from the ribs which, in turn, convey the weight to the piers from which they spring. The resulting thrust is met by the buttresses which, on the exterior, show above the roof of the triforium gallery. At the crossing additional ribs, or tiercerons, occur between the main diagonals in order to divide into two parts what would otherwise be too large a severy. Carved bosses mark the intersection of the diagonals and the meeting of the tiercerons with the ridge ribs. For greater lightness the severies are made of Guastavino tile faced with acoustic tile rather than being of stone in the traditional manner.

Additional stability is assured by the vaulting system over the aisles where tunnel vaults, slightly pointed, ribbed, and mutually buttressing, spring from arches that go from the piers to the aisle walls. The intersection of the high vaults with the outer wall is marked by a thin member, called a formeret, which springs from a slender shaft. The system, developed in the thirteenth century, of a vaulted ceiling resting on piers and buttresses made it possible to fill the entire wall area with glass. The Sainte-Chapelle in Paris is a notable example. In the Princeton Chapel, however, this system

4 The Apse

is not fully exploited, and the traceried windows are penetrations in the wall. This is more characteristic of the English practice, as are the "engine-turned" capitals of the pier shafts, each of which, on the side toward the nave, apparently carries its own vaulting rib.

Such precedent as there is for the architectural detail may be found in fourteenth century English buildings, such as Exeter Cathedral and the Octagon at Ely. This precedent has been very freely treated, and there has been no attempt at archaeological "correctness."

The architectural choir is unusually large and is intended, as in the English chapels, not only for the singers but for the entire congregation at a small service.

THE MATERIAL AND DIMENSIONS

THE exterior of the building is of Pennsylvania sandstone, trimmed with Indiana limestone. The interior work is of limestone, but a large part of the wall and the entire vault are faced with sound-absorbing tile. The floor is of limestone, and the aisles and the central space of the choir are of Aquia stone from the vicinity of Washington, D. C. No structural steel is used in the building save for the framing of the heavy lead-covered roof above the vaults. The footings and the foundations were poured in concrete, but above grade level the entire structure is masonry in the mediaeval tradition, without metal reinforcement. Provision was made in the construction for the possible addition of a central tower—the four great arches at the crossing are designed to carry the requisite load.*

During construction, in order to avoid a forest of scaffolding rising from the floor to support the wooden centering for the vaults, heavy steel i-beams were placed across at the level of the triforium gallery and later were skillfully withdrawn.

The dimensions of the Chapel are:

INTERIOR

> Extreme length, 249 feet
> Extreme width (nave and aisles), 61 feet 4 inches
> Extreme width (transepts and crossing), 93 feet 6 inches
> Extreme width (choir), 43 feet
> Extreme height (nave), 74 feet
> Extreme height (crossing), 78 feet 6 inches
> Extreme height (choir), 71 feet 6 inches

* According to Mr. Edward McMillan, at that time superintendent of Grounds and Buildings, a fault was discovered in the bedrock below one of the piers, a condition that required a carefully calculated bridging of the gap so as to insure stability.

5 South Facade

EXTERIOR

Extreme length (including buttresses), 277 feet
Extreme width (nave buttresses), 76 feet
Extreme width (transept buttresses), 64 feet
Extreme width (choir buttresses), 64 feet
Extreme height (ground to ridge), 121 feet

The architects of the Chapel were the firm of Cram and Ferguson of Boston. The builders were the Matthews Construction Company of Princeton.

THE EXTERIOR SCULPTURE

THE central feature of the west facade is the great tympanum over the main entrance. The subject is the majesty of Jesus Christ as described by St. John in the Apocalypse (Rev. 4 and 5). Christ, wearing the golden crown and supported by two angels, is seated. He holds the "Book," a large scroll, on which is the inscription: ΤΙΣ ΑΞΙΟΣ ΤΟ ΒΙΒΛΙΟΝ ΑΝΟΙΞΑΙ (Who is worthy to open the Book?). Small busts of the four and twenty elders form the double mandorla surrounding Christ. In the angles of the tympanum are the four beasts, the symbols of the Evangelists: the angel for Matthew, the lion for Mark, the ox for Luke, and the eagle for John. Below are the seven lamps burning before the throne. On the scroll may be seen small, round medallions, the seven seals (Rev. 6 and 7). These are to have mounted on them scenes symbolic of the seals and on the bosses of the main archivolt are to be little scenes from the Apocalypse, with Michael weighing the souls at the top. These have not, as yet, been commissioned. Above the main arch two angels hold a napkin with the crown of thorns, to suggest the Passion of Christ, just as the main sculpture on the tympanum represents His Triumph. The entire composition is thus a summation of the theme for the entire scheme of decoration of the Chapel. At the top of the upright between the two doors is the shield of the University, literally illustrating its motto: *Dei sub numine viget* (Under God's power she flourishes).

Plate 1

The tympanum of the northwest door represents the Annunciation. On the scroll held by the angel is inscribed: *et verbum caro factus est* (And the word was made flesh).

Over the southwest door the carving represents the Baptism of Christ. Across the foot of the panel is inscribed: *tu es filius meus dilectus in te complacuit mihi* (Thou art my beloved Son in whom I am well pleased).

Much of the ornamental sculpture on the exterior, such as the bosses of the high string-course above the clerestory around the entire chapel and the bosses that terminate the hood-molds of the larger windows, usually has no further significance, but on the east end angels are carved, and on the west facade are pine cones, a rebus for the Pyne family commemorated below.

THE INTERIOR

THE main vestibule is also, in a sense, a narthex. In the early church a place for catechumens not yet admitted to full membership in the church, the vestibule thus signifies the approach of man to the worship of God. In the Princeton Chapel, this vestibule has been incorporated within the mass of the building, and from it one may pass directly into the main central aisle, into the two side aisles, and to the stairs leading to the gallery above. Four small stained-glass windows (38–41, cf. pp. 99f.) give a rich note of color. On the wall just south of the main door is inscribed the prayer for the University, by Dean Donald B. Aldrich. It is used each Sunday in the service.

A PRAYER FOR PRINCETON

O ETERNAL GOD
THE CREATOR AND PRESERVER
OF ALL MANKIND WE BESEECH THEE
TO BESTOW UPON THIS UNIVERSITY
THY MANIFOLD GIFTS OF GRACE
THY TRUTH TO THOSE WHO TEACH
THY LAWS TO THOSE WHO LEARN
THY WISDOM TO THOSE WHO ADMINISTER
AND THY STEADFASTNESS TO ALL
WHO BEAR HER NAME
BIND US TOGETHER BY THESE
GRACIOUS INFLUENCES OF THY SPIRIT
INTO THAT FELLOWSHIP
WHICH CAN NEVER FAIL THE COMPANY
OF JESUS CHRIST OUR LORD
AMEN

Another inscription, from Psalm 100:2, over the entrance leading from the southwest door into the main part of the narthex, suggests the importance of the service of music in the tradition of the Chapel:

SERVE THE LORD WITH GLADNESS
COME BEFORE HIS PRESENCE WITH SINGING
WESTMINSTER CHOIR COLLEGE

The inscription, given by Lee Bristol, commemorates graduation ceremonies conducted annually in the Chapel by this institution.

The nave is entered from the narthex through three doorways. A lozenge is carved above each doorway as seen from the nave. In the central one, three interlaced circles representing the Trinity are carved at the center of the heavenly rose, described by Dante in Canto 33 of the Paradiso. In front of the circles is the figure of Christ, the Man of Sorrows. In the door to the right is the Lamb of God, in the door to the left the Dove.

6 The Vaulting, North Side →

7 The Milbank Choir

Within the body of the Chapel the aisles are relatively narrow, serving only as passageways and to give access to the pews (Pl. 21). Each aisle consists of five bays, the first, because of the narthex, corresponding to the second bay of the clerestory above. On the north side are four aisle windows (7–10 on the Plan), the fifth bay being taken up by the door leading in from the north porch. The south aisle has, on the other hand, five bays (32–36). Above the nave arcade runs a triforium gallery, corresponding to the level of the sloping roof over the aisles, and above the triforium are the windows of the clerestory (Pl. 6). There are six of these on each side along the nave (1–6; 26–31). The transepts have clerestory windows in their west (13 and 16) and east walls (17 and 18), and their level is carried into the choir by two windows high over the carved wooden organ cases (19 and 20).

Above the doorway in the north side are three shields representing the three chief religious centers for western Christendom: Jerusalem (a cross potence between four cross-crosslets), Rome (the keys of St. Peter), and Canterbury (a pall charged with cross-crosslets fitché, and a cross-crosslet in honor point). On the jambs of the door are carvings representing, to the left, the seven virtues and to the right the seven corresponding vices:

Humilitas (dove)	Superbia (peacock)
Caritas (horn of plenty)	Avaritia (miser)
Castitas (unicorn)	Luxuria (wolf)
Patientia (lamb)	Ira (woman with dagger)
Temperantia (centaur)	Voracitas (fish)
Misericordia (rose)	Invidia (bramble)
Diligentia (bee)	Desidia (pig)

The dedication of the Choir is recorded under the Great East Window in the following inscription:

The Milbank Choir
Plate 7

THIS CHOIR IS DEDICATED TO THE MEMORY OF ELIZABETH MILBANK ANDERSON
BORN DECEMBER 20, 1850, DIED FEBRUARY 22, 1921
ERECTED BY THE MILBANK MEMORIAL FUND, 1928

The choir is raised several steps above the general level, and at the east end stands the Holy Table, approached by three more steps. The five stalls behind the altar are used only when there is a celebration of Communion.

Choir Woodwork. Apart from the stained glass, the principal adornment of the choir is the beautiful woodwork. In design this furniture is without any particular precedent except that it may be said to be Gothic treated in a free and more modern manner. There are four rows of choir benches on each side, rising from the center to the sides. On all three sides of the choir, the wall row is divided into stalls and surmounted by a carved and traceried parapet carried on twisted colonettes. This parapet is raised over the five central stalls at the east end into a vaulted canopy, supported at each end by a niched pillar decorated with statuettes. Directly in front of these central stalls, at a lower level, is the Holy Table, which is simple in general lines but beautifully carved and molded. The organ cases rise from the stalls on either side of the entrance to the choir; underneath, on the south is the President's stall and on the opposite side, the organ console. Altogether the woodwork is carried out on a scale of sober magnificence rarely equaled in modern work. It is built entirely of pollard oak, centuries old, grown in Sherwood Forest, and in part probably dating back to the time of Robin Hood. The color and grain of the wood are so beautiful that no stain or varnish has been applied to it; the only finish is a coat of transparent lacquer to keep out the damp.

In front of the lowest row of benches, facing the center of the choir, is a parapet the ends of which, at each aisle, are decorated with carving and statuettes. Since the west portion of the choir is normally occupied by singers, the figures here are of personages associated with the history of music. On the right as one enters the Choir, the first three figures are Orpheus, St. Cecilia, and St. Ambrose. Orpheus was the musician in Greek legend who played so beautifully that even Cerberus, the guardian of the lower regions, was overcome. St. Ambrose traditionally is the originator of the plainsong of the Western Church, and St. Cecilia is the patron of music in general. Opposite, on the left, are Ptolemy, Pythagoras, and St. Gregory. Ptolemy is associated with the origin of Egyptian music, Pythagoras with Greek music. St. Gregory put into its later form the earlier music associated with St. Ambrose. He is shown with a whip since legend has it that he used to rehearse his choir whip in hand, ready to chasten any singer who performed incorrectly.

The portion of the choir beyond the seats alloted to the singers is, at special services, occupied by the faculty; here the statuettes are those of scholars. On the right the fourth figure is Aristotle; the fifth, King Alfred; and last, William of Wykeham, Bishop of Winchester, great builder and founder of Winchester School and New College, Oxford. Opposite, on the left, the fourth figure is St. Thomas Aquinas, the great scholastic philosopher; the fifth, Charlemagne; and last, the Venerable Bede, Anglo-Saxon teacher and historian.

The two supports at the ends of the central stalls behind the Holy Table are decorated with statuettes that indicate the line of succession of Teachers from apostolic days to the founding of Princeton University. On the left, at the top, are St. Peter, traditional founder of the Church at Rome, and St. Columba, the Celtic missionary. Below are St. Gregory and his missionary to England, St. Augustine of Canterbury. On the right, at the top, are Wycliffe and Calvin, and below them, Knox and Jonathan Edwards.

The angel figures in the parapet above the stalls hold small shields on which are various devices. Among these are the symbols of the four Evangelists: the angel for Matthew, the lion for Mark, the ox for Luke, and the eagle for John. In addition there are the pelican, symbolizing self-sacrifice; the chalice, symbol of the Holy Communion; the shell, symbol of Baptism; the cross with the letters to signify, "Jesus Christ conquers":

IC XC

NI KA

the crown of thorns and the nails, symbols of the Passion; and the three crowns, symbolizing the Trinity.

The medallions on the organ cases are personifications of the eight tones of Gregorian music.

All the choir furniture was built and carved by Irving and Casson, A. H. Davenport Company of Boston. It represents an outstanding example of American craftsmanship.

The Organ. The original organ, installed in the Chapel by the Skinner Organ Company, was one of the outstanding instruments of the 1920's. It was formally dedicated on the afternoon of Baccalaureate Sunday, June 17, 1928. The specifications and voicing details were drawn up by a number of leading organists of the period, including Charles M. Courboin and the late Alexander Russell, in consultation with Ernest M. Skinner and with G. Donald Harrison, who had been brought from England to act as a technical adviser. The instrument consisted of five divisions played from a console of four manuals and pedals. The south chamber contains the great, swell, choir, and pedal organs; the north chamber, the solo organ. The wind pressures vary from six to twenty-five inches. There were ninety-eight registers operating eighty-six speaking stops, and nearly 6,000 pipes. The pedal division includes three stops of 32-foot pitch.

In 1954 the organ was revised and planned by Carl Weinrich and G. Donald Harrison, now President of the Aeolian-Skinner Organ Company. The new pipe work demonstrates a change in organ design shared quite generally by all builders at that time. In 1957 a gallery organ, also built by the Aeolian-Skinner Organ Company, was dedicated. Located in the north triforium above the gallery, it is playable from the top manual of the console in the choir as an amplification of the chancel organ. It can be used also as a solo instrument.

The Pulpit. The exact provenience of the pulpit is not known, except that it came from the north of France and appears to date from the middle sixteenth century. It is of oak, richly carved. The style of the decoration is that of the French Renaissance of the period of Henry II. On the parapets and on the ramp are sculptured the signs of the zodiac, the labors of the months, and the sibyls, all in the manner of Jean Goujon.

The Lectern. The lectern is of carved oak and dates from the seventeenth century. It stood for some two hundred years in a church near Avranches, in Normandy, France. Just before the act which inventoried all church furniture in France as state property, this lectern was sold to the antiquarian, M. Bergevin. Mr. A. G. Grenfell, of England, a brother of Sir

Wilfred Grenfell of Labrador, purchased it for his school. President Hibben, in turn, secured it from Mr. Grenfell and presented it to the Chapel.

The Marquand Transept   As recorded in an inscription on the west wall, the transept to the north of the crossing is called:

THE MARQUAND TRANSEPT
IN GRATEFUL REMEMBRANCE OF
MARQUAND CHAPEL
THE GIFT OF HENRY G. MARQUAND
ERECTED 1881
DESTROYED BY FIRE 1920
IN MEMORIAM JAMES MC COSH
PRESIDENT OF THE COLLEGE
JAMES ORMSBEE MURRAY
FIRST DEAN OF THE COLLEGE
JOSEPH HENRY
PROFESSOR OF NATURAL PHILOSOPHY
ARNOLD GUYOT
PROFESSOR OF GEOLOGY AND PHYSICAL GEOGRAPHY
COMMEMORATED UPON THE WALLS OF
MARQUAND CHAPEL THEY WERE HONORED
IN THEIR GENERATIONS AND
WERE THE GLORY OF THEIR TIMES

Above the doorway on the west side of the transept are shields with the arms of the three oldest universities: Oxford (at the top), Paris (left), and Salamanca (right). On the jambs are carved, at the left, the seven liberal arts: grammar, dialectic, rhetoric, geometry, arithmetic, astronomy, and music; to the right, the seven gifts of the Holy Spirit: wisdom, understanding, counsel, fortitude, knowledge, godliness, and holy fear. Figures carrying appropriate symbols and lettering identify each.

Of the four flags that hang from the west wall, three are identified as follows from left to right: 1) flew over the U.S. Capitol for the first two years of Woodrow Wilson's Administration, 2) flown by the U.S.S. *Princeton V*, now in commission, 3) World War Service Flag, flown by U.S.S. *Princeton IV*, sunk in World War II. The arms of George Washington, who received the thanks of Congress in the "Old Prayer Hall" for his services in the War for Independence, also appear over the door on the west wall.

The central shield under the Great North Window bears the arms of the House of Nassau, to recall the fact that Nassau Hall, the original building of the college, was named in honor of William III, Prince of Orange-Nassau. The shield to the right bears the arms of the Channel Islands (the seat of the Marquand Family) and the shield to the left, the arms of George II of England, by whose charter the College of New Jersey was founded.

8 The Bright Pulpit →

9 The Hibben Garden

10 Ornamental Device on
East Facade

The central niche on the west wall of the transept is filled with the bronze relief portrait of President McCosh by Augustus St. Gaudens. The original relief was placed in the Marquand Chapel and perished in the fire of 1920. Fortunately, the sculptor's model had been preserved and a new relief could be made. The head of the original bronze was found in the ruins of the Marquand Chapel and is now in Firestone Library.

To the right, above the sanctuary of the apsidal chapel, is the seal of Henry G. Marquand, the donor of the former chapel; and to the left, a shield with a phoenix to symbolize the destruction and restoration of Mr. Marquand's gift. The oak paneling in the sanctuary of the apsidal chapel is a memorial gift, described below on p. 104.

The Crossing

On the bosses of the vaulting over the crossing are the following sculptures: on the central boss, the Trinity represented in the fifteenth century manner with the Father holding before Him Christ Crucified, while the Holy Spirit in the form of a dove flies between; on the bosses to the north and south, the legendary arms of the Twelve Apostles; to the east, two angels carrying a shield with the Lamb of God; to the west, two angels bearing again a shield with the letters IHS (Iesus Hominum Salvator).

The vaulting shafts in the transepts, on the west side, rest on corbels carved with the symbols of the Four Evangelists; the angel and eagle in the Braman Transept and the lion and the ox (intertwined in one corbel) in the Marquand Transept. At the ends of the transepts, arcades with stone seats (sedilia) lighten the effect of the wall structure.

The Braman Transept

The transept to the south of the crossing is named in honor of the first donor to the University Chapel Fund, Chester Alwyn Braman, whose name is inscribed on a stone in the south wall. The central shield, carved on the wall above the sedilia, shows the arms of Princeton University. To the right are the arms of Edinburgh University, the Alma Mater of John Witherspoon, and to the left, are those of Queen's College, Belfast, whence James McCosh was called to Princeton.

The flags on the south wall are, from left to right: 1) Queens University, Belfast; 2 and 3) Princeton University; 4) Edinburgh University, where two former presidents of Princeton studied, John Witherspoon and James McCosh. The banner that hangs in the corner is that of the University of Glasgow, where President McCosh also studied.

The staircase in the southwest corner of the Braman Transept leads to the Bright Pulpit, an outdoor pulpit built into the angle of the south transept and the nave. This memorial, together with the Hibben Garden by the north transept may be seen during a stroll around the outside of the Chapel.

Plate 8
Plate 9

THE STAINED-GLASS
WINDOWS

I N this description each window bears a number corresponding to the one shown on the Plan. The sequence begins on the north side with the windows of the clerestory (to the left as one enters the interior), returns to the aisle windows on the north side, and then goes on to the Marquand Transept, the Braman Transept, and the Milbank Choir. (Because the three great windows to the north, south, and east—14, 15, 21—are connected in meaning through their depiction of three aspects of Christ, the observer is urged to study them together, returning afterwards to note the relationship between windows 15 and 16 and to continue to window 17.) The sequence then proceeds via the south clerestory, reserving until last the windows of the south aisle. The subject matter here leads directly to the Great West Window (37), which portrays the Second Coming of Christ, the summation of all that has gone before.

The small windows in the narthex and at the stair landings leading up to the gallery above the narthex, as well as the glass in the south vestibule, are dealt with last.

The theme of all the glass in the main body of the Chapel is the life and teaching of Jesus Christ as recorded in the Four Gospels, together with the predictions and parallels of the Old Testament, and the subsequent influences of Christ's life and teaching in later times. The north aisle is devoted more especially to the life of Christ and the south aisle to His teaching.

Of the inscriptions that appear in the glass or on the wall adjoining it, only those pertaining to the iconography of the windows are included in the

Facing page:
The Great West Window,
The Second Coming of Christ

text. These are printed in italics to distinguish them from supplementary quotations. Inscriptions pertaining to the memorials appear in the Appendix.

As an aid in following the description, a diagram is provided for each of the eight largest windows—the four scriptural windows that mark the compass points of the Chapel and the four epic windows in the choir. Since each of the epic windows portrays a narrative, the order in which the artist intended the panels to be read is indicated by numbers at the lower left corner of each panel on the diagram, except for those panels in the Dante window which represent the circles, terraces, and heavens, already numbered in the Divine Comedy.

THE NAVE: NORTH SIDE

North Clerestory.
The Old Testament
(windows 1–6)

1. *First Bay.* Creation and Temptation

The three central lancets are occupied by the figures of Adam and Eve on either side of the Tree of Knowledge, about which Satan is entwined. The tempter is shown as a serpent with a human head. In the rose at the top is seen the Dove, the Spirit of God. Around the Dove are two inscribed bands. On the inner circle are the words: *And darkness was upon the face of the deep and the earth was without form and void* (Gen. 1:2). On the outer: *And the spirit of God moved upon the face of the waters and God said Let there be light and there was light, and God saw the light that it was good* (Gen. 1:2–4).

The two trefoils further dramatize the creation of light and dark. In the trefoil to the left:

Genesis 1:3–5, "And God said, Let there be light: and there was light . . . and God saw the light that it was good. . . . And God called the light Day."

In the trefoil to the right:

Genesis 1:4–5, ". . . And God divided the light from the darkness . . . and the darkness he called Night."

The four panels, from top to bottom in the left lancet, depict the events of the next four days of Creation:

Genesis 1:8, "God called the firmament Heaven."

Genesis 1:9–13, "And God said, Let the waters under the heaven be gathered together unto one place, and let the dry land appear. . . . And God said, Let the earth bring forth."

Genesis 14–19, "Let there be lights in the firmament of the heaven."

Genesis 1:21–23, "And God created great whales . . . and every winged fowl after his kind."

In the next panel, which is directly under the large figure of Adam, is shown the creation of man:

Genesis 2:7, "And the Lord God formed man."

In the next lancet are two panels. In the upper one, against the base of the Tree around which Satan is coiled:

Genesis 2:16–17, "But of the tree of the knowledge of good and evil, thou shalt not eat."

In the lower panel:

Genesis 2:20, "And Adam gave names to all cattle, and to the fowl of the air, and to every beast of the field."

In the next panel, directly under the large figure of Eve, is shown the creation of woman:

Genesis 2:22, "And the rib, which the Lord God had taken from man, made he a woman, and brought her unto the man."

The four panels, read from top to bottom in the right lancet, depict the Fall.

Genesis 3:7–8, "And the eyes of both of them were opened, and they knew that they were naked, and they sewed fig leaves together . . . and hid themselves from the presence of the Lord God among the trees of the garden."

Genesis 3:9–12, "And the Lord God called unto Adam . . . where art thou? And he said I was afraid and I hid myself . . . Hast thou eaten of the tree whereof I commanded thee that thou shouldst not eat? And the man said, The woman whom thou gavest to be with me, she gave me of the tree and I did eat."

Genesis 3:22–24, "And the Lord God said, Behold, the man is become as one of us, to know good from evil. Therefore the Lord God sent him forth from the garden of Eden and he placed at the east Cherubims and a flaming sword to keep the way of the tree of life."

Genesis 3:16–19, "Unto the woman he said, I will greatly multiply thy sorrow . . . and unto Adam he said, Because thou hast eaten of the tree, in sorrow shalt thou eat of it all the days of thy life, in the sweat of thy face shalt thou eat bread: for dust thou art and unto dust thou shalt return."

2. *Second Bay.* God and His Righteousness

The theme appears in the apex of the window. God the Father holds a Cross with the figure of the Crucified Savior beneath whom is the symbol of the Holy Spirit, the Dove. Around the circle are inscriptions from the Book of Job 36:3 and 5. *I will ascribe righteousness to my Maker and He is mighty in strength and wisdom.* In the flanking trefoils are angels. One holds the cuneiform tablets of the Code of Hammurabi, existing at the time of the Patriarchs, the other the Scales of Justice.

Five great figures of the patriarchal period occupy the lancets. From left to right: Abel, Noah, Abraham, Melchizedek, Job.

ABEL, firstborn of Adam and Eve, carries the lamb without blemish for sacrifice to God, whose acceptance is shown by the smoke rising from the altar. Above Abel is the martyr's palm, characterizing him as the first to lose his life for his faith. Below is Cain, his brother, from whose unacceptable sacrifice the smoke descends. In the background, the mark of Cain "And the Lord set a mark upon Cain lest any finding him should kill him" (Gen. 4:15). The implication is that vengeance belongs to God.

NOAH reaches up to take the dove back into the Ark, which rests on Ararat above Noah's nimbus. Below, the building of the Ark which has become the symbol of the Christian Church. At the side stand the unbelievers deriding Noah despite the storm cloud forming in the sky above.

ABRAHAM surrounded by the stars of heaven. The sand of the seashore below his feet symbolizes God's promise to make Abraham's seed into a great nation. On his scroll are the Star of David, the Latin Cross, and the Star and Crescent since he was the Patriarch of three great faiths: Hebrew, Christian, and Mohammedan. Above his head appears the hand of God in the act of changing the patriarch's name from Abram to Abraham, Father of many nations. In the panel below is Abraham about to sacrifice his son Isaac, at God's command. An angel arrests Abraham's hand and points to the ram caught in the thicket to indicate that man alone cannot atone for sin but only the blood of the Son of God.

MELCHIZEDEK, King of Salem and priest of the Most High God, in priestly attire. Above him is a kingly crown since he is the archetype of Christ, who is the King of Righteousness and Peace. Below, Melchizedek offers bread and wine to Abraham, who in return gives the royal priest his tithe, shown by the division of the bags into nine and one.

JOB, whose book seeks an answer to the suffering of the righteous. Satan tears away the robes that symbolize Job's wealth, comfort, and power, and boils appear on his exposed shoulder. On the banner is written *I know that my Redeemer liveth* (Job 19:25), the earliest record in the Bible of the knowledge of God's redemption. In the panel below, God permits Satan to test the faith of the righteous man.

3. *Third Bay.* The Law and Wisdom

The central panel of the window is occupied by MOSES, who holds the Tables of the Law. Above him is the Burning Bush, in which the angel of the Lord appeared but "the bush was not consumed" (Ex. 3:2). "God called to him out of the midst of the bush, and said, Moses. And he said, Here am I" (Ex. 3:4). In the panel below, inscribed *Law*, he receives the tables from the Lord.

At the extreme left is JACOB. Above him is the ladder of his vision, while in the panel below he wrestles with the Angel. "And there wrestled a man with him, and when he prevailed not he touched the hollow of his thigh (Gen. 32:25) and he said, "Thy name shall be called no more Jacob but Israel." Inscribed in the panel: *Strength*.

Between Moses and Jacob stands AARON with his rod that blossomed and was kept later in the Ark for a token (Num. 17:8). In the panel below is shown the worship of the golden calf. The inscription in the panel: *Transgression*.

To the right of Moses is SAMUEL who heard God's voice, represented by an angel with a trumpet; and below, in the panel inscribed *Anointment*, he anoints David.

The last panel on the right shows SOLOMON, with scepter, sword, and crown. Above him is his temple, and below is the scene of the Judgment of Solomon (1 Kings 3:16–27) inscribed *Wisdom*. In the rose at the top God is shown as the Lawgiver.

4. *Fourth Bay*. Jehovah as the Lord of Hosts.

In the rose at the top of the window is Jehovah, carrying a sword. The large figures represent, from left to right, the great captains of the Old Testament.

JOSHUA. Above him are the sun and moon which he commanded to stand still over Gibeon (Josh. 10:12–13). In the panel below there appears to him an angel carrying a sword (5:13).

GIDEON. Above him is the fleece of wool (Judg. 6:37) which he placed on the ground so that if the dew fell on the fleece only it would be a signal that the Lord would save Israel at his hands. And a second time, to make sure, he asked God that the dew should lie only on the ground, and it was so. In the panel below are his three companies bearing pitchers and lamps, and blowing upon trumpets as they cry, "The sword of the Lord and of Gideon" (Judg. 7:18).

DAVID, carrying sword and shield. Above him is a lyre, symbolic of his psalms. Below, he is shown slaying Goliath (1 Sam. 17:51).

SAMSON, bearing the jawbone of an ass, with with which he slew the Philistines. Above are the gates of Gaza, which he carried off (Judg. 16:3). Below he is shown rending apart the pillars of the temple. "And Samson said, Let me die with the Philistines. And he bowed himself with all his might, and the house fell upon the lords and upon all the people that were within. So the dead which he slew at his death were more than they which he slew in his life" (Judg. 16:30).

SAUL, armed with a spear. Above him is a crown, and in the scene below he is shown falling on his sword. Defeated by the Philistines, and knowing that his sons Jonathan and Aminadab were slain, he besought his armourbearer to kill him. "But his armourbearer would not; for he was sore afraid. Therefore Saul took a sword and fell upon it" (1 Sam. 31:4).

5. *Fifth Bay.* Individual Responsibility

The figures from left to right represent Nathan, Elijah, Ezekiel, Zechariah, and Jonah, on each of whom the Lord laid a charge to reprove wrongdoing. The panels below the figures illustrate significant events in their mission, and the symbols above them stand for further episodes as recorded in the Old Testament.

NATHAN (II Sam. 12:9) stands before David, reproving him for sending Uriah to die in battle so that Bathsheba could become his wife. Above Nathan is the knife which, in the parable, the rich man used to sacrifice the poor man's lamb instead of his own to feed the traveler.

ELIJAH, sent to reprove Ahab for worshiping Baal, prophesies a drought (I Kings 17ff) and is warned by God to flee away and hide ("I have commanded the ravens to feed thee"). Above the prophet appears the raven. Below, he is shown being caught up in the whirlwind and taken to heaven in a fiery chariot (II Kings 2:11).

EZEKIEL, sent to reprove the Children of Israel, saw the vision of God's glory. Shown below are cherubim, the wheels, the living creatures, the "wheel in the middle of the wheel" (Ezek. 1, 8, 10, 11:22). Above him the empty throne typifies the desolation of Jerusalem.

ZECHARIAH, exhorting to repentance, "saw a man riding upon a red horse" (Zech. 1:8), shown in the panel below. Above him is the Flying Scroll. "Then I turned and looked, and behold, a flying roll; the length thereof is twenty cubits, and the breadth thereof ten cubits" (Zech. 5:2). It was shown him by angels, and typified the curse that goeth forth over the face of the whole earth (Zech. 5:3).

JONAH, commanded to preach against the wickedness of Ninevah, shirked his responsibility and fled instead for Tarshish, but the ship on which he embarked was tempest-tossed. "And he said to them take me up and cast me forth into the sea . . . for I know that for my sake this great tempest is upon you" (Jon. 1:12). After Jonah had been swallowed by the "great fish" he repented, was cast up again, and proceeded to fulfil his mission. The ship is shown above his figure. Below he sleeps under the gourd-vine, which the Lord had prepared to shade him but which He then caused to wither. The people of Ninevah had repented and were forgiven, but Jonah was angry because of this. God reproved him saying, "Thou hast had pity on the gourd which came up in a night, and perished in a night. And should I not spare Ninevah, that great city?" (Jon. 4:10, 11).

Incorporated in the dedication below the window is a part of Psalm 15, "The Gentleman's Psalm" as it is known in some of the great English Public Schools. It is eminently appropriate to the subject of the window above.

LORD WHO SHALL DWELL IN THY TABERNACLE?

HE THAT DOETH THE THING WHICH IS RIGHT

AND SPEAKETH THE TRUTH FROM HIS HEART

HE THAT IS LOWLY IN HIS OWN EYES

HE THAT SWEARETH UNTO HIS NEIGHBOR AND

DISAPPOINTETH HIM NOT

AND HATH NOT TAKEN REWARD AGAINST THE INNOCENT.

WHOSO DOETH THESE THINGS SHALL NEVER FALL.

6. *Sixth Bay.* The Messiah Prophesied

The theme of the design is announced in the central tracery pieces at the top, the figure of Christ—Ecce Homo—surrounded by twelve flaming crosses to symbolize the twelve minor prophets. In the smaller tracery pieces are two angels with symbols of the Passion.

The four prophets who foretold the Coming of the Messiah—Hosea, Jeremiah, Isaiah, and Daniel, together with John the Baptist—appear in this order, each holding a scroll inscribed with a significant text, which is further emphasized by a scene from the life of Christ in the panel below. Above each figure appears his symbol.

At the left is HOSEA, whose mantle has fallen from his shoulder to symbolize Israel's infidelity. On the scroll is written: *For I desired mercy and not sacrifice. Hosea VI:6.* These words are further emphasized by the panel scene underneath, *S. Matt. 9:13,* where Christ quoted the same words to the Pharisees as he sat with publicans and sinners. Above Hosea in the six-pointed star is his symbol, the broken idol.

JEREMIAH holds a scroll inscribed: *Woe unto us that we have sinned, Lam. V:16,* written at the destruction of Jerusalem. In the scene below, Christ mourns over the city, *S. Matthew 23:27.* Above Jeremiah's head is his best-known symbol, the almond rod (Jer. 1:11, 12).

ISAIAH, in the center, dominates the entire group. Above him a seraph holds the coal of fire taken from the altar. *Isaiah VI:6–7.* On his scroll is the verse *The spirit of the Lord God is upon me. Isaiah LXI:1,* words read to the Pharisees in the Synagogue by Christ (*Luke 4:18*), as shown in the panel below.

DANIEL, in the fourth lancet, holds a scroll with the words: *One like the Son of Man came with the clouds of Heaven, Daniel VII:13,* which are almost identical with the prophetic words of Christ before the High Priest (Matt. 26:64). The lower panel suggests this prophecy and shows the High Priest rending his garments at such blasphemy. The symbol above the Prophet's head is the lion in the six-pointed star.

ST. JOHN THE BAPTIST, whose symbol is the Lamb on the Book, holds the scroll: *Behold the Lamb of God which taketh away the sin of the world.*

S. John 1:29. In the panel below he is represented baptizing Christ in the river Jordan. An angel holds the robe of Christ.

The color scheme, a well-balanced contrast of cool and warm colors, suggests the sustained good will and hopeful good tidings of the prophets.

North Aisle.
The New Testament
(windows 7–10)

7. *Second Bay.* The Annunciation and the Nativity

In the upper register is a row of figures with John the Baptist, the Precursor, in the center. Above him is the Lamb of God. To the left, the Three Kings see the Star over Bethlehem; to the right is the Angel of the Annunciation, with the word *Ave* (Maria). The Holy Ghost descends in the form of a dove.

In the lower register the center shows the Nativity, the Infant Christ with Mary and Joseph. The town of Bethlehem and the Star appear behind and above them. To the left the Three Kings make their offerings as they adore the Christ; to the right are the shepherds also in adoration.

8. *Third Bay.* Scenes from the Life of Christ

In the upper register are depicted the three temptations of Christ. The angel in the central panel refers to the second temptation. "He shall give his angels charge concerning thee; and in their hands shall they bear thee up" (Matt. 4:5–7).

In the lower register, Christ drives the money-changers from the temple, transforms water into wine at the marriage at Cana, and preaches from a boat on the Sea of Galilee.

9. *Fourth Bay.* Scenes from the Life of Christ

In the upper register Christ heals the demoniac, restores the sight of the blind man, and heals the leper. Below, the three panels represent the Miracle of the Loaves and Fishes—the Feeding of the Multitude.

10. *Fifth Bay.* Scenes from the Life of Christ

The center of the upper register represents the Transfiguration. To the left, Peter sinks into the sea on which he had attempted to walk to his Lord, and on the right Christ stills the storm on the Sea of Galilee.

The three lower panels represent the Entry into Jerusalem on Palm Sunday, and lead to the final scenes of Christ's life as depicted both in the two small windows in the Marquand Chapel (11–12), and in the Great East Window (21).

THE MARQUAND TRANSEPT

Each of the two windows shows twelve scenes from the life of Christ in the period from the Last Supper to the Ascension. These form a continuation of the scenes in the north aisle and with them make up a historical sequence.

11. *Left Bay.* Events of Holy Week

Beginning at the lower left and reading up, one sees the Last Supper, the Agony in the Garden of Gethsemane, the kiss of Judas, Christ before the Priests, Christ before Pilate, and Christ despoiled of His raiment. In the right lancet, again reading up, one sees the Crowning with Thorns, Christ mocked, Pilate washing his hands, Christ falling under the weight of the Cross, Simon helping Him, and the Crucifixion.

12. *Right Bay.* Events of Holy Week

In the second window, again in the same order, one sees Christ on the Cross with the Virgin and St. John below, Christ and the Centurion, Judas returning the betrayal money, the Descent from the Cross, the Pietà, and the Entombment. In the right lancet of the window are depicted the Angel at the Tomb, Christ appearing to Mary Magdalene ("Noli me tangere"), the Doubting of Thomas, the Appearance to the Disciples in the Upper Chamber, the Supper at Emmaus, and the Ascension.

In the rose above the left-hand window is an angel with the Chalice, the cup from which Christ drank at the Last Supper, and above the right-hand window, the Crown of Thorns worn by the Crucified Christ, with the letters IHS (Iesus Hominum Salvator).

13. *West Clerestory.* Friendship

This window replaces one of the transept windows of the former Marquand Chapel and is to be regarded as a part of the nave clerestory cycle. In the two top panels of the central lancets, David carrying his sling faces Jonathan. Read from the top downwards, the panels at the left illustrate episodes in the story of their friendship and in David's relationship with King Saul (1 Samuel): 1) *Warning.* Jonathan shoots an arrow to warn David to flee from Saul. 2) *Jealousy.* Saul attacks David. 3) *Solace.* David plays on the harp before Saul. 4) *Prowess.* David slays a lion. Read from the top downward, the panels at the right illustrate: 5) *Loyalty,* 6) *Retribution,* 7) *Love,* and, under the figure of Jonathan, 8) *Esteem.*

The North Window (14)   14. *The Great North Window.* Christ the Martyr

This is one of the four largest windows in the Chapel, which are richest in iconography as well as in color. They form the climax of the decoration and pictorial thought. Each is based on a quotation from the teaching of Christ recorded in large letters either in the glass or carved in the stone under the window. His words are illustrated both by scenes of His own life and by those figures from history who have exemplified the quality implied in the quotation. Each window is a unit in itself, while together they record in a permanent and vivid form the cardinal qualities of a real and complete existence according to Christ: Endurance, Truth, Love, and Life. The theme of this window is stated in the text carved in the stone beneath: *He that shall endure unto the end, the same shall be saved* (Mark 13:13).

Christ is the central figure of the window. He is clad in the martyr's red, wears the crown of thorns and holds the palm of martyrdom. Below is the inscription, *Ecce Homo* (Behold the Man). To His right and left are the archangels Gabriel and Raphael. Beneath the figure of Christ is Michael, clad in armor and holding a flaming sword. The panel just below represents him weighing the souls. Those who attain salvation are carried up by angels, seen in the two lateral roses at the top of the window, to find peace at last in the bosom of Abraham, who occupies the central rose at the top. In the small panels below the three central figures are shown the Flagellation of Christ, Christ Crowned with Thorns, Christ Carrying the Cross. In the pair of lancets to the left of Gabriel are St. Sebastian, with the scene of his martyrdom below (the executioner's sword would not cut him) and St. Stephen, first martyr, who is shown in the panel below being stoned. In the pair of lancets to the right are St. Lawrence, carrying the gridiron on which he was martyred, with a scene of his martyrdom below; and St. Christopher, carrying the Infant Christ. In the panel beneath he carries the fully grown Christ, and thus the sins of the world.

In the lower range are figures of martyrs or other personages noted for their heroic endurance or steadfastness: Cardinal Mercier, Archbishop of Louvain (World War I), Chevalier Bayard "Sans peur et sans reproche"; St. George with a small panel just above showing him slaying the dragon; St. Theodore, also slaying a dragon in the form of a crocodile; Ste. Jeanne d'Arc; and St. Thomas à Becket, martyred at Canterbury.

The seven small panels across the base of the window show symbols associated with the Savior. In the very center is the Lamb of God signifying sacrifice. Then, reading from the left, the peacock for incorruptibility; the chalice, scourge and crown of thorns for His Passion; the lion for courage; the phoenix for resurrection. In the small lights in the tracery at the top of the window are cherubim and the letters Alpha and Omega, "I am the beginning and the end."

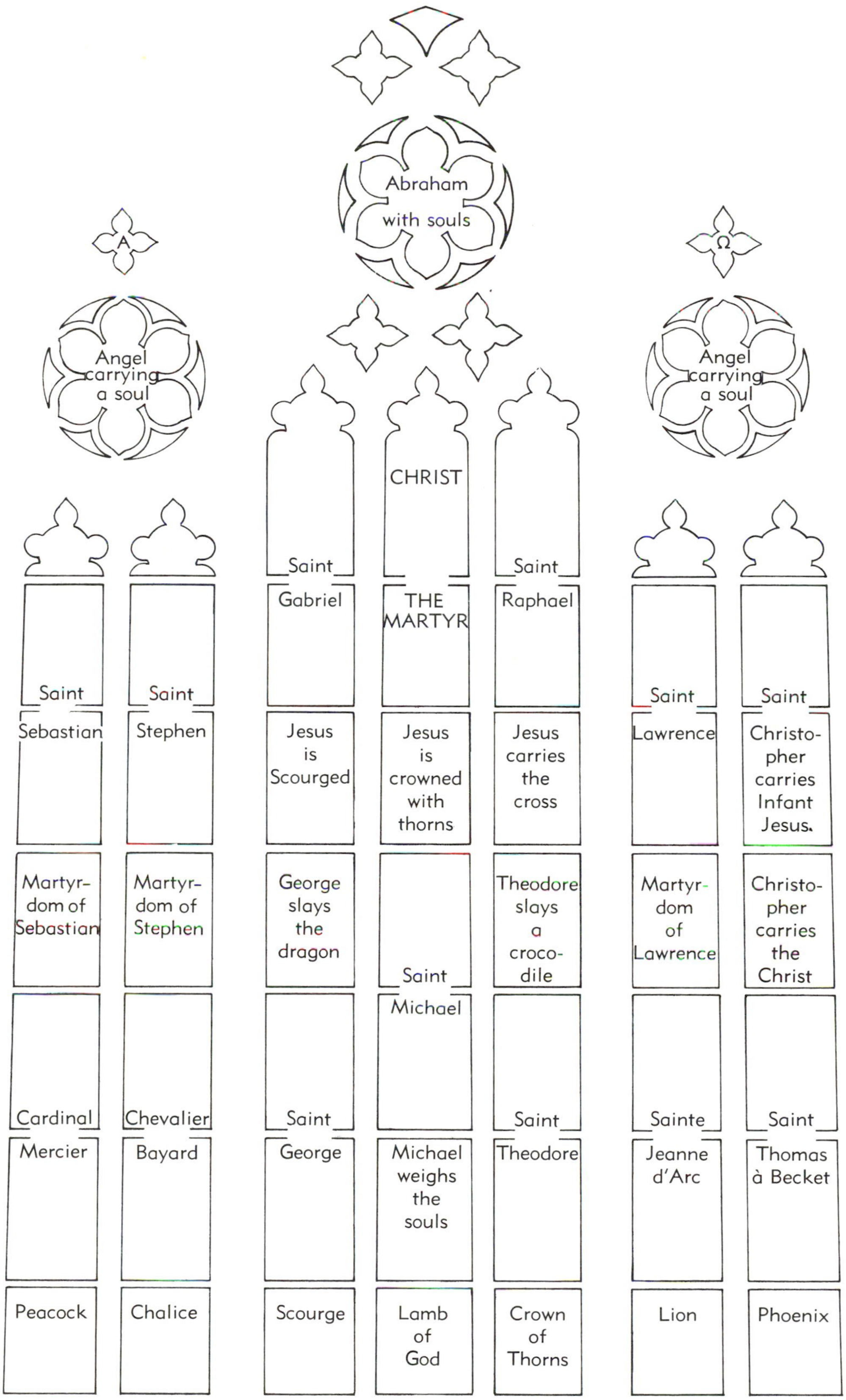
Abraham with souls
A
Ω
Angel carrying a soul
Angel carrying a soul
CHRIST
Saint Gabriel
THE MARTYR
Saint Raphael
Saint Sebastian
Saint Stephen
Jesus is Scourged
Jesus is crowned with thorns
Jesus carries the cross
Saint Lawrence
Saint Christopher carries Infant Jesus.
Martyrdom of Sebastian
Martyrdom of Stephen
George slays the dragon
Saint Michael
Theodore slays a crocodile
Martyrdom of Lawrence
Christopher carries the Christ
Cardinal Mercier
Chevalier Bayard
Saint George
Michael weighs the souls
Saint Theodore
Sainte Jeanne d'Arc
Saint Thomas à Becket
Peacock
Chalice
Scourge
Lamb of God
Crown of Thorns
Lion
Phoenix

The Great North Window: Christ the Martyr

THE BRAMAN TRANSEPT

The South Window (15)   15. *The Great South Window.* Christ the Teacher

In the stone beneath the widow is carved: *And ye shall know the truth and the truth shall make you free* (John 8:32).

The chief figure is Christ the Teacher, wearing a blue mantle and carrying the Book. On the left is St. Paul; on the right is St. John, the great mystics of the New Testament. Above, in the central rose, Christ sits enthroned while there proceed from Him seven doves, the seven gifts of the Holy Spirit, wisdom, understanding, counsel, fortitude, knowledge, piety, holy fear.

Immediately below the figures are three panels representing Christ before Pilate: *What is truth?*; Christ at Emmaus: *Via et Veritas et Vita* ("I am the way, the truth and the life," John 14:6); and the Doubting of Thomas. In the small rose above and to the left of St. Paul is a representation of his vision on the way to Damascus. The corresponding rose on the right shows the scene on the Island of Patmos, where St. John is supposed to have written his Gospel. Near St. Paul is his symbol, the book and the sword, and near St. John is his symbol, the eagle.

On either side of the mystical writers stand the practical teachers; to the left of St. Paul, St. Peter, holding his keys and to the right of St. John, St. James the Less. Below St. Peter is a panel representing Christ saying to Peter: *Feed my lamb*s; and below St. James, a scene showing him writing his epistle. The outermost figures of the upper row are two Christian scholars. On the left is Clement of Alexandria, the speculative thinker. Below, he is shown teaching. On the right is Jerome of Bethlehem. Below, he is shown translating the Vulgate (accuracy insures preservation of the text).

The five large figures in the lower row are the great preservers or examples of the Christian truth. In the center is St. Augustine of Hippo, greatest father of the Church. The panel beneath him shows his conversion at Ostia, through the influence of his mother Monica, to the truth of Christianity, *Tolle, Lege* (Take up and read). On the left stands St. Benedict, preserver of ancient writings as shown in the panel immediately above him. To the right of Augustine is St. Francis of Assisi, the seeker for truth through the imitation of Christ, even to receiving the stigmata symbolized by the crucifix he holds. In the small scene above he preaches to his brethren and his friends, the birds. The two figures in the left lancets are Alcuin, preserver of the Bible and master of the Schools of Charlemagne, and John of Salisbury, Bishop of Chartres, a humanist of the twelfth century and the most learned man of his time. To the right of St. Francis stand Erasmus, scholar of the Reformation, and John Witherspoon, sixth president of Princeton, philosopher, theologian, and teacher of political history.

The seven panels at the foot of the window represent the seven liberal arts: arithmetic, geometry, astronomy, rhetoric, dialectic, grammar, and music.

35

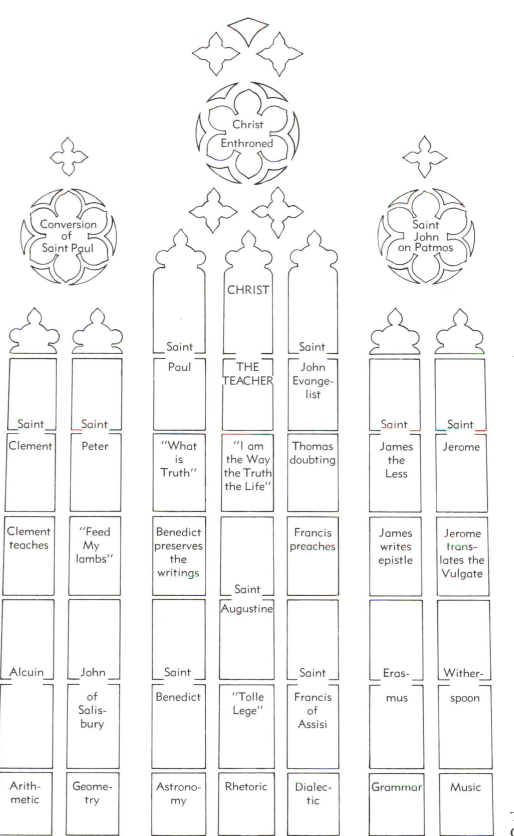

The Great South Window:
Christ the Teacher

West Clerestory
(window 16)

16. *West Clerestory.* Christ's Disciples and Their Modern Counterparts

In the two top panels of the central lancets, Christ is shown sending out his disciples: "Go therefore and teach all nations." In the remaining panels at the left appears Gerard Groote, Roman Catholic reformer of Dutch origin. In the two central panels at the bottom are Martin Luther, preaching at the left and writing at the right. The bottom panel at the right shows John Knox, preaching to Mary Queen of Scots, who is dressed in red. Above are John Wesley and George Whitfield, and at the top is Whitfield, preaching on the steps of Nassau Hall.

The door in the east wall of the Braman Transept leads to the south vestibule, which provides access to the vestry and the eastern portion of the crypt. At the head of the stairs to the crypt is a memorial window (44), and over the southeast door the tracery is enlivened by stained glass, also a memorial (45). Both are described below, p. 105.

THE CROSSING AND THE CHOIR CLERESTORY

The Book of Psalms
(windows 17–20)

On the east side of the two transepts and in the choir above the organ cases are four windows which together illustrate aspects of the great themes in the Book of the Psalms. The windows are composed of numerous little scenes that are literal illustrations of verses from the Psalms, or are scenes from the life of Christ suggested by the verses.* The four lancets in each window are to be read from left to right, and the three panels in each lancet from top to bottom.

17. *North Transept.* Psalms 147, 148, 150

The psalmist David appears in the rose. All creation, the heavens, the earth, and creatures on the earth, are exhorted to praise God.

First lancet. *Alleluia.* Figure of an angel
    1. *Let them praise the name of the Lord: for he commanded and they were created.* Ps. 148:5
    2. *He sendeth out his word: he causeth his wind to blow and the waters (to) flow.* Ps. 147:18
    3. *Kings of the earth and all people.* Ps. 148:11 *Let everything that hath breath praise the Lord.* Ps. 150:6

Second lancet. *Alleluia.* Angel
    1. *Praise him all his angels: praise him all his hosts.* Ps. 148:2 *Praise him ye heaven of heavens.* Ps. 148:4
    2. *He exalteth the horn of his people, the praise of his saints even the children of Israel.* Ps. 148:14

* These scenes are very difficult to decipher and in some instances the description is speculative.

3. *Young men and maidens* (148:12) *Praise the Lord for his name alone is excellent.* Ps. 148:13

Third lancet. *Alleluia.* Angel

1. *Praise him sun and moon. Praise him all ye stars of light.* Ps. 148:3. *Praise God.*
2. *Let the saints be joyful in glory. Let the praises of God be in their mouths.* Ps. 149:5–6
3. *Old men and Children* Ps. 148:12. *Let them praise his name. His glory is above the earth and heaven.* Ps. 148:13

Fourth lancet. *Alleluia.* Angel

1. *Praise ye the Lord. Praise ye the Lord from the heavens. Praise him in the heights.* Ps. 148:1
2. *Fire and hail; snow and vapours, stormy wind fulfilling his word.* Ps. 148:8 *praising God*
3. *Judges praise the Lord* Ps. 148:11. *Let everything that hath breath praise the Lord.* Ps. 150:6

In the stone below this window is the following inscription:

Praise ye the Lord
Praise ye the Lord from the Heavens
Praise him in the Highest, Praise him all his Angels
Praise him all his hosts.

18. *South Transept.* Psalm 107

David appears in the rose. The Redeemed are exhorted to observe God's manifold providence to man in various vicissitudes—the wanderer, the captive, the sick.

First lancet

1. *Thirsty their soul fainted.* Ps. 107:5
2. *And he led them forth.* Ps. 107:7
3. *He turneth the land into barrenness.* Ps. 107:33–34

Second lancet

1. *They rebelled against the word.* Ps. 107:11. Scene of Adam and Eve expelled from the garden.
2. *He brought them out of darkness.* Ps. 107:14. Christ heals the blind.
3. *He maketh the storm a calm.* Ps. 107:29

Third lancet

1. *He brake their bands in sunder.* Ps. 107:14
2. *They cried unto the Lord.* Ps. 107:13
3. *He sent his word and healed them.* Ps. 107:20. Scene of the nativity.

Fourth lancet

1. *He satisfieth the longing soul.* Ps. 107:9. Christ is shown with a naked man kneeling before Him.
2. *That they may prepare a city.* Ps. 107:36
3. *They sow the fields.* Ps. 107:37

19. *The Choir, North Side.* Psalms 22 and 23

In the rose above: Christ. To the left, an angel with a viol; to the right, an angel with a pipe. In this window, two great psalms, one of despair and one of confidence, are juxtaposed as they are in the book itself.

First lancet

1. *They gaped upon me with their mouths as a ravening and a roaring lion.* Ps. 22:13
2. *Our fathers trusted in thee and thou didst deliver them.* Ps. 22:4
3. *He hath not despised nor abhorred the affliction of the afflicted.* Ps. 22:24

Second lancet

1. *All they that go down to the dust shall bow before him.* Ps. 22:29
2. *My God why hast thou forsaken me? Why art thou so far from helping me?* Ps. 22:1. Christ in Gethsemane.
3. *And all the kindreds of the nations shall worship before thee.* Ps. 22:27

Third lancet

1. *I am poured out like water and all my bones are out of joint.* Ps. 22:14. Christ is crucified.
2. *They parted my garments among them and cast lots upon my vesture.* Ps. 22:18
3. *But thou art he that took me out of the womb.* Ps. 22:9. Scene of nativity.

Fourth lancet

1. *He maketh me to lie down in green pastures, He restoreth my soul.* Ps. 23:2 and 3
2. *Though I walk through the valley of the shadow of death I will fear no evil.* Ps. 23:4
3. *Thou preparest a table before me in the presence of mine enemies.* Ps. 23:5

20. *The Choir, South Side.* Psalm 91

Christ as Abraham appears in the rose. To his left and right are angels with censers. The well-known psalm of deliverance is depicted.

First lancet

1. *He is my refuge, in him will I trust.* Ps. 91:2. Figure of King David.
2. *His truth shall be thy shield and buckler.* Ps. 91:4. Angel gives sword and shield.
3. *Thou shalt not be afraid for the terror by night.* Ps. 91:5. Moses and the death of Egypt's firstborn.

Second lancet

1. *Thou shalt not be afraid for the pestilence.* Ps. 91:6. Job is blest by God and the devil is cast out from him.
2. *Only with thine eyes shalt thou behold.* Ps. 91:8. A figure looking into the pit of Hell.
3. *They shall bear thee up.* Ps. 91:12. Christ supported by angels.

Third lancet

1. *There shall no evil befall thee.* Ps. 91:10. Elijah being taken to heaven.
2. *A thousand shall fall at thy side.* Ps. 91:7. Noah and the Ark.
3. *He shall give his angels charge over thee.* Ps. 91:11. The angel with Tobias.

Fourth lancet

1. *Thou shalt tread upon the lion and the adder.* Ps. 91:13. Christ standing upon the lion and the adder.
2. *Because he hath known me I will deliver him.* Ps. 91:14. Christ lifts two souls into heaven.
3. *Therefore will I deliver him and honour him.* Ps. 91:15. Joseph sold into slavery.

THE MILBANK CHOIR

IN a description of the Chapel Professor A. M. Friend wrote, "The chief decoration of the choir is the magnificent series of stained-glass windows. The glass in the great chapel is so designed that it becomes deeper in color and more serene in harmony as it approaches the east end. The windows of the choir with their resonant and richly toned color form a solemn ensemble which is the completion of the pictorial splendor of the whole interior. Here the dominant quality is a blue of deep transparence throughout which glint and move subsidiary colors, the myriad little figures in the medallions which compose in their varied patterns the fine fabric of this vitreous decoration."

The subjects depicted in the Great East Window and in the two windows in the first bays (19, 20) bear a close relationship in that the former, the summation of the life and teaching of Christ, celebrates the love of God for man and of man for God; the latter, two psalms of David, are closely associated with Christ's Passion. The remaining four windows illustrate four great Christian Epics (below, pp. 45f.) which typify the search of man for the knowledge of the love of God.

21. *The Great East Window.** The Love of Christ

The East Window (21)
Plates 11 and 12

The Great East Window represents Christ as the embodiment of Divine Love. Emerging from the delicate pattern of the sensitive little panels, this figure, clad in the red robe of the martyr, stands serene and steadfast, visible the entire length of the Chapel. At His right is *Virgin Mary Mother,* and at his left is *Saint John Evangelist,* His disciple and friend, the author of the Gospel of Love. In one hand John holds a quill and in the other a scroll

* The description of this window as originally written by A. M. Friend has been augmented for the sake of completeness.

40

The Great East Window:
The Love of Christ

on which is written *and the word was made flesh and dwelt among us* (John 1:14). The variations of the blue in the robes of the Virgin and St. John move ever closer to the quiet red of the central figure.

At the foot of the window are the words of Christ which contain the essence of His teaching to His Apostles: *A new commandment I give unto you that ye love one another as I have loved you* (John 13:34). These words were spoken at the Last Supper and therefore this scene is represented in the central position in the glass. In the triangular spaces above the heads of the Disciples is written: *By this shall all men know that ye are my disciples— if ye have love one to another* (John 13:35). Immediately below the scene, Christ washes Peter's feet: *The servant is not greater than his Lord* (13:16).

At the ends of the lunate table at which the disciples are seated are the letters A and Ω ("I am the beginning and the ending" Rev. 1:8); below the figure of Christ, as He sits between Peter and John, is the monogram XPC. Christos.

The symbols of the Evangelists appear below Mary (Matthew, Mark) and below St. John (Luke, John). Across the three central lancets at and just below the level of the scene of the Last Supper are twelve shields charged with legendary coats of arms associated with the Twelve Apostles. From left to right they are: a cross between stars for James the Less, three spear points for Thomas, a flaying knife for Bartholomew, and a basket with two loaves of bread for Philip. The next four shields are at a higher level: a saltire for Andrew, crossed keys for Peter, an eagle for John, and three scallop shells for James. The last four, at the level of the first set are: an angel for Matthew, thirty pieces of silver for Judas, a ship for Jude, and two fishes for Simon the Canaanite.

Surrounding the scene of the Last Supper and in the tall lancets at either side of the window are thirty-three panels showing scenes from the life and teachings of Christ which illustrate the central theme of the window, love. Below and to the left of Christ washing Peter's feet, Mary sits at Christ's feet in adoration while her sister Martha is busy with serving: *A certain woman named Martha received him into her house* (Luke 10:38). To the right Mary Magdalene anoints the feet of Jesus with precious ointment: *Her sins are forgiven for she loved much* (Luke 7:47). Below, immediately above the large inscription, are three scenes illustrating the parable of the Good Samaritan, told by Christ to the lawyer who asked, after receiving the two commandments of love, "And who is my neighbor?" *A certain Samaritan as he journeyed / came to where he was and when he saw him / he had compassion on him* (Luke 10:33).

At the base of the two left lancets are the two commandments: *Thou shalt love the Lord thy God* (Matt. 22–37) represented by Moses with the Tablets of the Law, and *Thou shalt love thy neighbor as thyself* (Matt. 22:39),

11 The Great East Window,
The Love of Christ

12 The Great East
Window, detail

represented by Christ. In the panels above these Christ calls Peter and Andrew from their nets: "Follow me and I will make you fishers of men" (Matt.
4:19), and parallel with this his command to Matthew, seated at the place
of toll: *Follow me* (Matt. 9:9). Above is the contrast between the widow who
gives her mite, *But she of her want did cast in all that she had* (Mark 12:44),
and the rich young man who sorrowfully refuses to part with his wealth:
Sell whatsoever thou hast and give to the poor (Mark 10:21, Luke 18:22).
In the next panels above, Christ as the Good Shepherd finds the lost sheep:
I have found my sheep which was lost (Luke 15:6), and the father welcomes
home the prodigal son: *For this my son which was dead and is alive again*
(Luke 15:24). Then are seen the Pharisee and the humble publican praying
each in his own fashion: *He that humbleth himself shall be exalted* (Luke
18:14). To the right is Christ receiving the little children: *Except ye become
as* (little) *children ye shall not enter into* (the kingdom of) *Heaven,* (Matt.
18:3). In the next tier above, Jesus raises his friend Lazarus from the dead;
Jesus wept—Behold how He loved him (John 11:35–36), and Peter at the
sight of his Master on the shore impetuously casts himself into the sea to go
to him: *Simon Peter did cast himself into the Sea* (John 21:7). Above comes
Mary Magdalene early on Easter morning to the sepulcher and finds the
stone rolled away: *And seeth the stone taken away from the sepulcher* (John
20:1). Peter and John run to the tomb to seek their Lord but John outran
Peter and came first to the sepulcher: *The other disciple did outrun Peter*
(John 20:4).

The two lancets at the right are likewise composed of panels in pairs
which point out similarities and contrasts in Christ's life and teaching. The
inner lancet depicts in seven scenes the teaching of Christ in Matthew 25,
which describes the judgment according to the two commandments on which
hang all the law and the prophets; "Inasmuch as ye have done it unto the
least of these my brethren ye have done it unto me." In the background in
each case sits Christ in brilliant white robes silently looking on. Parallel with
each scene there is in the outer lancet one illustrating a similar episode in
the actual life of Christ. Thus at the bottom one man serves food to another:
I was an hungred, and ye gave me meat (Matt. 25:35). To the right Levi
invites Jesus to the feast in his house: *And Levi made him a great feast in
his own house* (Luke 5:29). Above, *I was thirsty and ye gave me drink*
(Matt. 25:35). Parallel is the scene of Christ and the woman of Samaria at
the well: *Give me to drink* (John 4:7). Again, is represented: *I was a stranger
and ye took me in* (Matt. 25:35), with Zacchaeus in the sycamore tree inviting
Christ to his house: *This day is salvation come to this house* (Luke 19:9).
Above, *Naked and ye clothed me* (Matt. 25:36), while to the right Nicodemus
and Joseph of Arimathea clothe the naked body of Jesus taken from the
cross: *Then took they the body and wound it in linen clothes* (John 19:40).
I was sick and ye visited me (Matt. 25:36) is contrasted with the agony in

the Garden of Gethsemane; Jesus says to the sleeping disciples, *Could ye not watch with me one hour?* (Matt. 26:40). Above, *I was in prison and ye came unto me* (Matt. 25:36) is contrasted with the scene of Peter denying Christ even after following Him into the High Priest's palace: *Before the cock crow thou shalt deny Me thrice* (Luke 22:61). At the top is the judgment. *He shall set the sheep on His right hand but the goats on the left* (Matt. 25:33), but in the outer panel those very sheep are entrusted to the same frail Peter who had denied his Lord: *Simon son of Jonas lovest thou me* (John 21:16), "Feed my sheep."

The culmination of the whole window is the Crucifixion in the great rose: *And I, if I be lifted up from the earth, will draw all men unto me* (John 12:32). In the rose at the left the Risen Christ appears to the two Marys; and at the right, to the Disciples on the way to Emmaus, thus to all women and to all men. It was the desire of the donors of the window that it should represent Love, and the theme is most fully exemplified by Christ's sacrifice for mankind: *Greater love hath no man than this that a man lay down his life for his friends. Saint John XV:13,* an inscription that appears in the glass just below the large figures of Christ, His Mother, and St. John the Evangelist.

In the small quatrefoils are: above, the symbol of God the Father at the left, and God the Holy Ghost at the right. In the two quatrefoils below are, on the left, the Tables of the Law, symbol of the Old Testament, and, at the right, the symbol of the New Testament. In the smaller quatrefoils to either side are, at the right, a veiled sun, and at the left a veiled moon.

The Four Epic Windows (22–25)

Each of these represents a cycle of one of the great Christian Epics. The window at the far end on the left (northeast), depicts the Divine Comedy of Dante. Next to this is Malory's Le Morte d'Arthur. The window at the far end on the right (southeast) depicts Milton's Paradise Lost and beside it is Bunyan's Pilgrim's Progress.

These epics were chosen because each represents a quest for reality conducted through the hazards of this life and attained finally by the power of Divine Love. The small rose at the top of each window shows the mystical vision of Christ, which is the goal of each epic. The windows mark a sustained effort to symbolize, in an accompaniment of color and light, the great expressions of Christian aspiration and attainment. The following descriptions of the windows are based very largely on the program of the artist, which was carefully written out as the designs progressed. Many of the legends are difficult to read without a glass, but they, and the scenes that go with them, will amply repay prolonged study, not alone for the subject matter but also for an appreciation of the painstaking research and imagination of the artist.

46

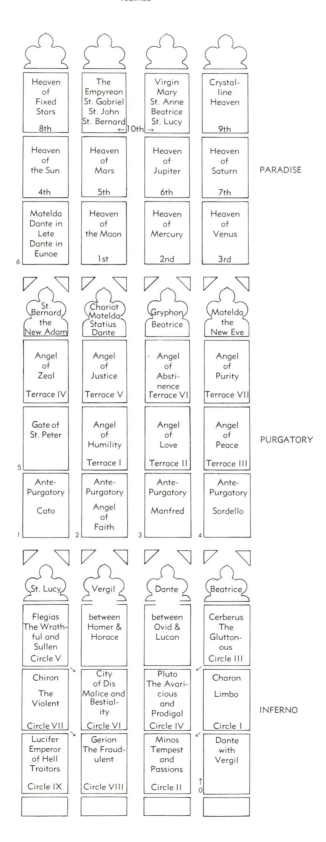

The
Mystic Rose

Beatrice

Heaven of Fixed Stars 8th	The Empyrean St. Gabriel St. John St. Bernard ←10th→	Virgin Mary St. Anne Beatrice St. Lucy	Crystal-line Heaven 9th	
Heaven of the Sun 4th	Heaven of Mars 5th	Heaven of Jupiter 6th	Heaven of Saturn 7th	PARADISE
Matelda Dante in Lete Dante in Eunoe	Heaven of the Moon 1st	Heaven of Mercury 2nd	Heaven of Venus 3rd	

St. Bernard the New Adam	Chariot Matelda Statius Dante	Gryphon Beatrice	Matelda the New Eve	
Angel of Zeal Terrace IV	Angel of Justice Terrace V	Angel of Absti-nence Terrace VI	Angel of Purity Terrace VII	
Gate of St. Peter	Angel of Humility Terrace I	Angel of Love Terrace II	Angel of Peace Terrace III	PURGATORY
Ante-Purgatory Cato	Ante-Purgatory Angel of Faith	Ante-Purgatory Manfred	Ante-Purgatory Sordello	

St. Lucy	Vergil	Dante	Beatrice	
Flegias The Wrath-ful and Sullen Circle V	between Homer & Horace	between Ovid & Lucan	Cerberus The Glutton-ous Circle III	
Chiron The Violent Circle VII	City of Dis Malice and Bestial-ity Circle VI	Pluto The Avari-cious and Prodigal Circle IV	Charon Limbo Circle I	INFERNO
Lucifer Emperor of Hell Traitors Circle IX	Gerion The Fraud-ulent Circle VIII	Minos Tempest and Passions Circle II	Dante with Vergil	

The Dante Window:
La Divina Commedia

22. This is the most complex of the four epic windows, filled as it is with allegory and symbolism of Dante's vision. Through it the figure of Beatrice Portinari, his inspiration, is the moving force. In the Inferno his guide is Vergil, sent by her to conduct Dante. The Latin poet accompanies him through the successive stages of Purgatory but it is Beatrice herself, whom Dante thinks of as Divine Philosophy, who explains, heaven by heaven, the ascending steps of Paradise. To his sight she grows ever more resplendent until, her mission accomplished, she is no longer needed allegorically as he approaches the understanding of Divine Love. Under the guidance of St. Bernard he finally beholds the Mystic Rose.

The imagination displayed by the artist in incorporating in the medium of stained glass so much of the essence of the greatest poem of the Middle Ages is a veritable tour de force.

The window is divided into three tiers of lancets which symbolize Inferno, Purgatorio, and Paradiso. The arrangement of the poem is preserved as much as is consistent with the medium. In the Inferno the direction is in declining lines, from higher to lower; from left to right in Purgatory, and vertical in Paradise. Above, in the tracery are symbolized the Mystic Rose, the Spheres, and the Angelic Hierarchy.

The Bottom Tier

The order in which the panels are to be read is as follows:

```
   V           III
     ↘       ↙
   VII  VI  IV  I
       ↘     ↙
     IX  VIII  II
```

Through the base of the four lancets in the bottom tier runs an inscription that characterizes the treatment of the entire window:

> *La gloria di colui che tutto move*
> *Per l'universo penetra, è risplende*
> *In una parte più, è meno altrove.*
> (Paradiso, Canto I, lines 1–3)

"The glory of Him who moves everything penetrates through the universe, and is resplendent in one part more and in another less." (Norton's translation)

Heraldry and various symbols—animals, circles, and triangles—add a personal significance to these lines. There appear, from left to right, the arms of Dante, St. Lucy (a lamp for spiritual guidance), the Guelfs (a red lily), four prominent families of usurers known to Dante and mentioned in the Inferno—Gianfigliazzi, Ubbriachi, Scorvini of Padua, Giovanni Buiamonte—Ghibellines (a white lily), St. Thomas Aquinas, and Beatrice Portinari.

Panels of the Bottom Tier

Introductory Panel 0

mi ritrovai per una selva oscura
"I found myself in a dark wood." (Canto I, line 2)

Plate 13

Dante is shown asleep in the "Dark Wood," with an empty scroll, his still unwritten poem, emblazoned with his traditional arms and marked with seven P's (*peccati*) for his consciousness of sin, anticipating the marks made on his forehead by the Angel's sword as he enters Purgatory. Confronting him are three beasts—Leopard (Lust), Lion (Pride), and Wolf (Avarice). Above his head are the "Three Ladies from Heaven"—St. Lucy (Illuminating Grace), the Blessed Virgin (Divine Mercy), and Beatrice (Divine Philosophy). The Greyhound with the crown recalls Dante's mystical *Veltro*, symbol of the perfected Empire for which he longed. Nine flames worked into the design stand for the nine circles of hell, and an hourglass, half spent, recalls the words: "In the midst of the journey of my life."

Opposite Dante stands Vergil who points upward and holds a scroll with his name—*Publius Vergilius Maro*. Behind, and above him at the left is his symbolic lyre.

Circle I

Lasciate ogni speranza, voi ch'entrate.
"Leave every hope, ye who enter!" (Canto III, line 9)

Framed under hell's gate is Charon, the dark ferryman, with his boat of lost souls. As Dante passes through this gate he reaches Limbo, where dwell the unbaptized, indicated by small figures of children and the virtuous pagans: Aeneas, Hector, Caesar, and Saladin, shown by coats of arms; Aristotle, Plato, and Socrates, by books inscribed with their respective names. In the low center is the *nobile castello* (Canto IV, line 106), residence of the "great spirits of Antiquity." The indented battlements are indicative of the Ghibelline party, and the flame above the castle recalls Dante's description of Limbo as lit by a "glowing radiance" (Canto IV, lines 68–69).

Circle II

Nessun maggior dolore
"There is no greater woe" (Canto V, line 121)

Minos is identified by an inscription, and stands for tempest and the passions. Below Minos is the shield of Achilles attacked by a wild boar. The ounce and the he-goat are also symbols of unbridled lust.

The shields of the lovers, Paolo Malatesta and Francesca da Polenta, both slain by her jealous husband, are above the small figures of the two.

13 The Dante Window,
Introductory Panel

Circle III

per la dannosa colpa della gola
"For the pernicious fault of gluttony" (Canto VI, line 53)

Gluttony is represented by the strange beast Cerberus, from whose three heads emanate cold, rain, and snow. In this, as in all the other circles, are the small figures of Dante and his guide Vergil, who may here be seen below the uplifted right hand of Cerberus. The shield (lower right) is that of Ciacco, nicknamed "pig" by his fellow Florentines. The fox and pig are both symbols of gluttony.

Circle IV

Mal dare e mal tener lo mondo pulcro
ha tolto loro . . .
"Ill-giving and ill-keeping have taken from them
the beautiful world . . ." (Canto VII, lines 58–59)

Here are the avaricious and prodigal (Avari—Prodighi), twin evils. *Pluto*, demon god of wealth, rules this circle, and beasts with miters, tiaras, and crowns, who represent clerks, popes, and other officials, jostle each other as they vainly roll great burdens. Dante recognized no one in this circle.

Circle V

Gran regi . . . come porci in brago
"Great kings . . . like swine in mire" (Canto VIII, lines 49–50)

In this circle are the wrathful and sullen. *Flegias*, in Greek mythology king of Boeotia, had a daughter loved by Apollo, and in revenge he burned the god's temple at Delphi. He is represented holding a torch to recall the event, as he stands in his boat on the river Styx, while Dante and Vergil stand near the prow. Crowned pigs wallow in the mire. The porcupine symbolizes evil anger, and the shield is that of Filippo Argenti, the "raging Florentine," whom Dante cursed and Vergil pushed away from the boat.

Circle VI

D'ogni malizia . . . Ingiuria e . . . il fine
"Of every wickedness . . . injury is the end" (Canto XI, lines 22–23)

The fiery red city of Dis comprises the whole of Nether Hell and forms a complete circle about the Pit. It stands for sins of malice and bestiality where the will is actively involved. Neither Dante nor Vergil were admitted until an angel opened the gate for them. Above the walls is a small bust of Erine, shown as a Medusa head. A hydra symbolizes heretics, and a frog stands for pride in unbelief. At the left of the scene is Farinata degli Uberti, leader of the Ghibelline party in Florence and a man of wisdom and valor. The sword of victory and the Florentine Lily identify him as, on one occasion, the savior of the city. The shields are those of Cavalcanti, a noted

Epicurean, Ubaldini, Cardinal and a violent Ghibelline, and Pope Ana-
stasius II, reputed to have been a heretic.

Circle VII
di mezzo . . . E il gran Chirone
"He in the middle . . . is the great Chiron." (Canto XII, lines 70–71)

The centaur *Chirone* with bow and arrow chastizes the violent—those
who are violent against others or against themselves. At the upper left is
the Harpy, symbol of suicide. The shields above are those of Obizzo da Esti,
violent against others although his reputation for cruelty and vice may have
been exaggerated; Pier della Vigna, a suicide, and thus violent against himself; Capaneo, one of the Seven against Thebes who defied Zeus and thus
was violent against the god; and Andrea de Mozzi, Bishop of Florence, who
practiced unnatural vice and thus stands for violence against nature. Below,
on money bags, where Dante said they belonged, are the arms of four usurers
who were violent against art: Gianfigliazzi (a lion's mask), Ubbriachi (a
goose), Scrovigni of Padua (a sow in brood), and Giovanni Buiamonte (three
beaks of eagles). Over them crawls a bestial dragon devouring a trefoil, the
symbol of beauty.

Circle VIII
Fatto v'avete Dio d'oro e d'argento
"Ye have made you a god of gold and silver" (Canto XIX, line 112)

The fiend *Gerion*, whose cattle Hercules carried off in one of his labors,
presides over this circle as a personification of fraud. Vergil shows Dante
the deep chasms called Malebolge (Evil Pouches) in each of which a different
kind of fraud is punished. Elsewhere (in Circle VII) Dante associates coats of
arms with purses rather than shields, and the artist represents the chasms by
money pouches as more appropriate to display the devices of the shades en-
countered in this circle. The following can be recognized: Venedico Caccia-
nemico, pander, who sold his own sister to the Marchese Obizzo d'Este;
Thais, flatteress; Nicholas II, simoniac; Michael Scot, soothsayer and sor-
cerer; Malebranch, barrator; Priappas, hypocrite; Agnello Brunelleschi,
thief; Evildo da Montefeltro, evil counsellor; Pier da Medecina, sower of
scandal and schism; and Capocchio, falsifier. The fox and the mermaid
stand for fraud and seduction.

Circle IX
Lo imperador del doloroso regno
"The Emperor of the woeful realm" (Canto XXXIV, line 28)

The ninth circle of Hell is the frozen lake of Cocytus, which fills the
bottom of the pit and holds the souls of the traitors. In the upper part of
the panel is the figure of Lucifer, the fallen Archangel. As Emperor of
Hell he had three faces to represent the antitype of the Godhead. The center

one is red for impotence, the one to the right is yellow for hate, and the one on the left is black for ignorance. These contrast with the divine attributes: Power, Love, and Wisdom. Three pairs of bat wings and three chilling circles complete the symbolism, along with four frozen circles and representative coats of arms. Beneath the jaws of the three faces are the shields of the archtraitors: Judas (center), traitor of churches, marked with the thirty pieces of silver for which he betrayed his Lord, and to left and right, the shields of Brutus and Cassius, betrayers of empire, each showing the dagger of the assassin. In the first, outer ring, named Caina for Cain, the first traitor, is the shield of Alessandro degli Alberti, murderer of his brother in a quarrel over their inheritance; in the second ring, named Antenora for the traitorous Trojan, the shield of Bocca degli Abati, betrayer of the Florentines at the battle of Montaperti. In the third ring, named Ptolomea for that Ptolemy whose treachery is recounted in the Book of Maccabees, is the shield of Friar Alberic (Alberigo de Manfredi), who killed his brother and nephew at a feast to which he had invited them.

Large Figures of the Bottom Tier

The large figures at the top of the central lancets show the poets in Limbo, the gray-green flame of which is suggested in the color of their symbols. Vergil stands at the left, between Homer and Horace; Dante is to the right flanked by Ovid and Lucan. The Roman poet is identified not only by a shield with the symbolic lyre but also by the inscription: *Divinus poeta nostra Virgilius**—"our Divine poet, Virgil." Across his figure and that of his two companions is inscribed:

> *la bella scuola*
> *Di quei signor dell'altissimo canto*
> "The fair school of that Lord of loftiest song" (Canto IV, line 95)

At his feet are three books, symbolic of the ancients who inspired him—Homer, Lucretius (center), and Hesiod—*Omero, Lucretio, Esiodo.*

Dante is identified by his family coat of arms overhead, and by the inscription: *Il tua fidele* "Thy faithful one." Below him are the works of the philosophers that greatly influenced him, Socrates, Aristotle, and Plato, each inscribed with the proper name. He bears a scroll with three clouded suns, recalling a part of the days he spent in the Inferno. As in the group to the left, an inscription runs across him and his companions:

> *Ch'esser mi fecer della loro schiera,*
> *Si ch' io fui sesto tra cotanto senno.*
> "For they made me of their band
> So that I was sixth amid so much wisdom" (Canto IV, lines 101–2)

The shields of both Vergil and Dante are supported by eagles to signify the soaring splendor of their songs.

* Elsewhere the spelling Vergil is used.

St. Lucy, *Illuminata Grazia*, stands between a lamp and a seraph in the top of the outer left lancet, just above Circle v. On the other side, above Circle iii, is Beatrice, *Divina Filosophia*, with her family coat of arms and, at her left, a small seraph.

The tracery pieces at the top of the bottom tier contain designs of beasts and stars for the triumph of faith over evil.

The Middle Tier

The Purgatory of Dante is depicted as a mountain, situated at the antipodes of the earth from Jerusalem. It consists of several stages or terraces where those who occupy them, for a longer or shorter time, are purged of their sins and finally received Divine pardon. It is a place of penance, not punishment.

In this tier, the panels read from left to right and from bottom to top. The four lower panels represent Ante-Purgatory, the first on the second row is the gate of St. Peter, the entrance to Purgatory itself. The seven terraces follow. Blue, "that sweet color," forms the background for each of the panels. Growing forms are green, with developing leaves; and the ascending direction of the dominating lines is that of the mountain, Aspiration.

1. Ante-Purgatory

Liberta va cercando, che e si cara.
"He seeketh Liberty which is so dear" (Canto i, line 71)

Cato is the apostle of Liberty, and in the Middle Ages he was the accepted type of natural, moral virtue. Around his head are four brilliant stars representing the cardinal virtues: Prudence, Justice, Fortitude, and Temperance. He guards the shore and the mountain. Souls await ascent, and Dante is girded with a green rush to signify humility. The eagle on the shield symbolizes Cato.

2. Ante-Purgatory

In exitu Israel (Canto ii, line 46)
L'uccel divino (Canto ii, line 38)

The Angel of Faith guides across the river the ship of the newly redeemed dead, who are singing a hymn that symbolizes their deliverance in terms of the deliverance of the Israelites from Egypt. The white star is a symbol of faith. "The bird divine" shone so brightly that Dante was compelled to cast down his eyes.

3. Ante-Purgatory

sì non si perde
che non possa tornar l'eterno amore.
"One is not so lost that the Eternal love cannot return" (Canto iii, lines 133–34)

Manfred, tardy in repentance, is accompanied by angels of hope. He was the natural son of the Emperor Frederick and had been excommunicated by Pope Clement IV. Killed at Benevento, he had not had time to repent. The shields are those of Belacqua, named "The Slothful," and Tarlati, who made his peace with God at the last moment.

4. Ante-Purgatory
Salve Regina
"Hail Queen" (Canto VII, line 82)

This is the valley of the Princes, guardian angels, clad in green, who are shown driving away serpents. Between them is Sordello, who greeted Vergil as a fellow Mantuan. The famous troubador was negligent in repentance. The shields are those of Rudolph of Hapsburg and King Ottocar of Bohemia, enemies on earth but here reconciled. The third shield is that of Alphonso III of Aragon, grandson of Manfred, "a good lord, redoubted by Christians and Saracens alike" (Villani, Chron. VII, 103).

5. The Gate of St. Peter
quivi e la porta
"here is the Gate" (Canto IX, line 90)

This forms the entrance from Ante-Purgatory to the seven succeeding terraces. Here sits the gray-robed angel of Obedience, whose silver and gold keys of judgment and absolution open the gate to Dante and whose sword marks on his forehead seven P's (*peccati*) for his sins. These are indicated on the shield in front of his small figure as he stands with Vergil at the lower left of the panel. Above is the "Eagle with feathers of gold poised in the sky" (Canto IX, lines 19–20), which the poet saw in his dream. Leading up to the gate are three steps. The first is white for Contrition; the second, dark purple, cracked in the form of a cross, for Confession; and the third, flaming red porphyry for Amendment. At the top, right, is a lozenge with a lamp for St. Lucy. It was she who carried Dante up to the gate. Below is a shield with the Keys of St. Peter.

Terrace I
Beati pauperes spiritu
"Blessed are the poor in spirit" (Canto XII, line 110)

The Angel of Humility (*umilta*) places a heavy burden on a figure to subdue his pride. The lion below is the beast of Pride (*superbia*), especially related to tyrants and tyranny. The shields are those of Provenzano Salvani, proud of his birth, who performed a public act of humility to secure the release of a friend, and Umberto Aldobrandesco, representing pride of Dominion. Dante's shield has now but six P's. One was expunged by the Angel of Humility.

Terrace II, where envy is purged
Beati misericordes
"Blessed are the merciful" (Canto XV, line 38)

The Angel of Love (*amor*) ties a bandage over the eyes of the penitent to suggest the temporarily closed eyes of those who had misused them on earth. At his feet the serpent, beast of envy (*invidia*), is actively coiled suggesting power. The shields are those of Rinier da Calboli, a distinguished Guelf of Forli, and of Guido del Duca, who represents the type of envy that resents joy in others. Only five P's remain on Dante's shield, one more having been expunged by the Angel of Love.

Terrace III. The penance of the wrathful
Beati pacifici
"Blessed are the peacemakers" (Canto XVII, lines 68–69)

The Angel of Peace (*pace*) in the clouds of smoke that Dante saw. Below is the beast of Evil Anger, the leopard (*ira mala*). The shield is that of Marco Lombardo, a generous man but hot-tempered. The Angel has removed one more P from Dante's shield, so that only four remain.

Terrace IV. The penance of the slothful
qui lugent . . . beati
"Blessed are they that mourn" (Canto XIX, line 50)

Below the Angel of Zeal (*studio*) is the Swine, the beast of Sloth (*accidia*), symbol of defective love. The shield is that of the Abbot of San Zeno, but nothing is known of him or of his sins of slothfulness. Only three P's remain on Dante's shield, one more being expunged by the Angel of Zeal.

Terrace V, where the covetous are fettered face downward
Beati qui sitiunt justitiam
"Blessed are they which do thirst after justice" (Canto XXII, line 5)

The Angel of Justice (*giustitia*), weeps as he holds the scales. Avarice (*avarizia*) is represented by a wolf. The shield is that of Hugh Capet, founder of the Capetian dynasty, "the root of the evil plant." He was distinguished by his lust for temporal power. Statius joins Vergil and Dante, who admired him greatly as the Poet of the "Silver Age." He tells the two that he had become a Christian by reading Vergil's writings. On Dante's shield only two P's are left.

Terrace VI, where the Gluttonous do penance by starvation
Beati qui esuriunt justitiam
"Blessed are they which do hunger after justice" (Canto XXIV, line 151)

The Angel of Abstinence (*astinenza*) stands with an inverted fruit tree, signifying chastisement (Canto XXII, line 133). Below him is the beast of Gluttony. The shields are those of Forese Donate (lower right), a close friend of Dante, Bonagiunta (lower left), a fellow poet and a hard drinker, and Martin IV (upper left), a native of Tours, who died of a surfeit of eels stewed in Vermaccia wine. The Angel has expunged another P from Dante's shield so that only one remains.

Terrace VII, where the souls of the lustful are purged
Beati mundo corde.
"Blessed are the pure in heart" (Canto XXVII, line 8)

The Angel of Purity (*puritas*) cleanses Dante's shield with fire. "And I saw spirits going through the flame." The leopard is the beast of Lust. At the upper left a cherubim with a flaming sword suggests welcome back to Eden, the Earthly Paradise, symbolized through the tops of the four lancets. St. Bernard, on the left, represents the New Adam, and is a symbol of the contemplative life. He is the counterpart of Matelda (possibly Matelda of Hackeborn, a mystical writer who may have influenced Dante), the New Eve, symbol of the active spiritual life. She appears at the top of the right hand lancet. Flanking the two figures are the small symbols of the four Evangelists, angel, ox, lion, and eagle.

In the two central spaces are the Gryphon, symbol of the hypostatic union of the two natures of Christ; the Chariot, symbol of the Church, and Beatrice. Around the Chariot are seven candlesticks—the Gifts of the Spirit —to signify the Active Life. The Gryphon is surrounded by Seven New Testament Books to signify the contemplative life. At the wheels of the chariot follow Matelda, Statius, and Dante, who wears the miter crown of Freedom given him by Vergil. Dante's guide through Inferno and Purgatorio no longer appears for we have now entered that realm of revealed truth which is beyond Vergil's understanding and belongs to Beatrice.

The Top Tier

Dante's Paradise consists of ten heavens, nine in motion and one fixed. Over each of the moving spheres presides one of the nine orders of intelligences, which shine as concentric circles of light around the Divine Essence in the Tenth Heaven. In each panel that illustrates a moving heaven, Dante and Beatrice, his spiritual guide, appear in a small roundel held by one of these presiding angels. The rest of the panel is filled with the arms or shields of those with whom Dante converses or of whom he is told. As he and his guide advance from sphere to sphere, Beatrice becomes increasingly resplendent since every sphere is a step toward the Tenth Heaven, the Paradise of Saints and Angels, where the soul attains perfect knowledge, supreme love, and infinite blessedness in its union with God. An inscription runs across the base of the four lowest panels:

La divina bonta . . . ardendo in se, sfavilla
Si, che dispiega le belleze eterne

"The Divine Goodness . . . burning in itself, so sparkles
that it displays the eternal beauties."
(Paradiso, Canto VII, lines 64–65)

6. The Two Rivers

On either side of Matelda (cf. p. 56) Dante is represented standing in a river: *Lete*, which takes away the memory of sin; and at the right, *Eunoe*, the river that restores the memory of every good deed. Both rivers issue from the mystical fountain of the Grace of God.

First Heaven
Cielo della Luna (Heaven of the Moon)

In this first heaven Dante finds those who broke their vows, some against their will, or who performed their vows imperfectly. Assigned to this lowest sphere, they are nonetheless content in that "In His will is perfected our peace" (III, 85), words which appear across the base of the two central panels of the top lancet, representing the Tenth Heaven. Cf. below.

Second Heaven
Cielo di Mercurio (Heaven of Mercury)

This is the realm of those who did great things for humanity but whose motives were mixed with personal ambition, love of fame or of honor. The arms are those of Justinian, who addressed Dante as a member of the Church Militant (Canto VI), and the Roman Eagle, symbol of the Empire, won to Christianity by Justinian.

Third Heaven
Cielo di Venere (Heaven of Venus)

This is the realm of purified lovers who have striven but have failed from lack of temperance. The arms on the right are those of Carlo Martello (Charles Martel), grandson of Charles I of Anjou and friend of Dante. He stands as the symbol of the sensual man, accompanied nevertheless by a generous ardor. He was called "Gentle ruler." On the left are the arms of Folco (Foulquet of Marseilles), troubador and poet, an "uplifted lover" who retired to a monastery and later became bishop of Toulouse in 1205. "Now they are seen as brilliant lights moving circle-wise, hidden in the rays of their own joy."

Fourth Heaven
Cielo del Sole (Heaven of the Sun)

This is the realm of great teachers and doctors who illuminated the world by example and precept. They are the champions who lead the army of Christ against darkness and heal spiritual disease. The shields are those of St. Francis, seen by Dante as the new embodiment of the spirit of Christ on earth (left), St. Dominic (right), characterized by his great learning; St. Thomas Aquinas (upper left), most famous of scholastic theologians; and Albertus Magnus (upper right), the master of Aquinas. "These spirits appear now as surpassingly vivid lights, as so many suns apparent against the burning background of the Sun because more brilliant than it."

Fifth Heaven
Cielo di Marte (Heaven of Mars)

This realm is the scene of Dante's encounter with the souls of those who have died for the faith. Illustrated are the arms of William, Count of Orange (right), celebrated in the Old French Chansons de Gestes for his defence of Christendom against the Saracens and Godfrey of Bouillon (left), leader of the First Crusade.

Sixth Heaven
Cielo di Giove (Heaven of Jupiter)

This is the sphere of just rulers whose spirits appear as golden lights, singing like a flock of birds, as they form themselves successively from the initial letter of Monarchy **M** through the shape of the Florentine Lily into the Celestial Eagle of the Empire, indicating Dante's faith in the Empire. The Eagle above is the symbol of Divine Justice. The arms are those of William II of Sicily, surnamed "The Good," who was praised for his just and righteous rule.

Seventh Heaven
Cielo di Saturno (Heaven of Saturn)

This is the realm of those who passed their lives in holy contemplation. The shields are those of Contemplative Spirits: St. Peter Damian and St. Benedict, whose lives emphasize Temperance.

Eighth Heaven
Cielo Stellato (Heaven of Fixed Stars)

This realm is presided over by Cherubim, who represent Wisdom and spread the knowledge of God. Flaming books signify that their special work is illuminating. The shields are those of Peter, James, John, and Adam, who are related to the Cherubim as symbols of Faith, Hope, Charity and of this Heaven as the celestial counterpart of Paradise. The shield of St. Dominic, at the bottom, represents Divine Wisdom, and that of St. Francis symbolizes Divine Love. The small figures of Dante and Beatrice in the roundel are encircled by myriads of shining lights typifying the Celestial counterpart of the Garden of Eden.

Ninth Heaven
Cielo Cristallino (The Crystalline Heaven)

This last material sphere, the Primum Mobile, is presided over by Seraphim as images of Divine Love. On either side of the Seraph are flaming hearts, the symbols of that love. The special work of the Seraphim is perfecting. The shield is that of St. Francis of Assisi (Divine Love).

Tenth Heaven

Sua volunta e nostra pace
"His will is our peace" (Across the base of the two lancets)

This, the Empyrean, is the true Paradise of vision, comprehension, and fruition—the Paradise of Saints and Angels. Man's will is here in union with the Universal Good, his intellect in possession of Universal Truth. Here are the River of Light and the Fountain of Truth from which Dante drinks and is enabled to see the vision of God and all the spiritual things which the blessed behold. This Heaven is illustrated by figures of SS. Gabriel, John, and Bernard (in the left lancet), who completes the task of Beatrice and who, as the poet's last guide and counsellor, has above him the shield of Dante. In the right lancet are shown the Blessed Virgin Mary, St. Anne, Beatrice, and St. Lucy. Above Beatrice is the disk of light with the Fountain of Truth, to suggest her mission of Divine Philosopher throughout the poem. Figures of little children appear in both groups to suggest their place in the Mystic Rose. The shields on the left are those of Christ, as the New Adam, Moses, St. Peter, and St. John Evangelist while on the right are those of Rachel, Beatrice, St. Anne, and St. Lucy.

The Tracery of the Top Tier

The tracery is designed as a comprehensive symbol of the Ten Heavens, culminating in the Mystic Rose. In the four lower pieces are the four torches mentioned in the Crystalline Heaven—the four Cardinal Virtues. Ten stars in circles of color and light symbolize the Heavens; a small figure of Beatrice, enthroned in the tracery piece beneath the quatrefoil, symbolizes the spirit dominating the poem. In her robes of white, green, and red are symbolized the three Theological Virtues, Faith, Hope, and Charity. In the quatrefoil at the very top of the window is the Mystic Rose, the figure of Christ in the symbol of the Trinity, as King, with orb and scepter. Around Him are the closing words of the poem:

L'amor che move il sole e l'altre stelle
"The love that moves the sun and the other stars" (Canto XXXIII, line 145)

A white six-pointed star to His left suggests Adam, a gold five-pointed star to His right, St. Peter, a blue-white one below, Moses, and a red, above, St. John the Divine. These recall the allegory in which the old and new beginning and the old and new law are expressed.

23. Written in the fifteenth century by Sir Thomas Malory, the tales are bewildering in number and variety, but as we become familiar with Le Morte d'Arthur, we recognize the great themes that give it unity. The love

NORTH BAY.
MALORY,
LE MORTE D'ARTHUR (23)

60

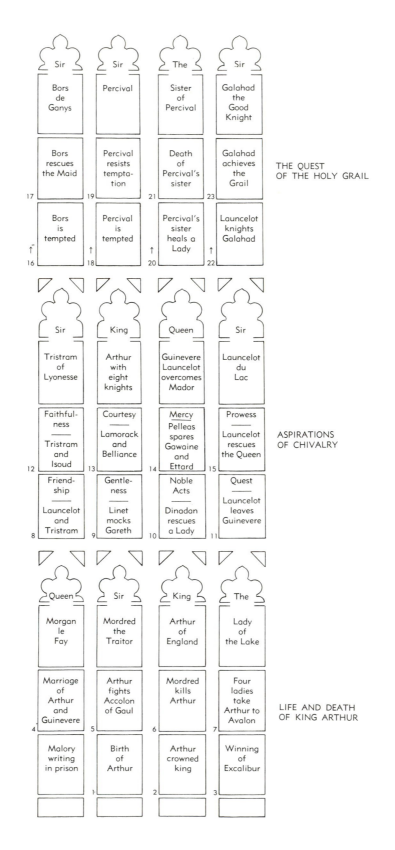

The Vision of Christ

Sir Bors de Ganys

Bors rescues the Maid

Bors is tempted

17 16

Sir Percival

Percival resists temptation

Percival is tempted

19 18

The Sister of Percival

Death of Percival's sister

Percival's sister heals a Lady

21 20

Sir Galahad the Good Knight

Galahad achieves the Grail

Launcelot knights Galahad

23 22

THE QUEST
OF THE HOLY GRAIL

Sir Tristram of Lyonesse

Faithfulness
—
Tristram and Isoud

Friendship
—
Launcelot and Tristram

12 8

King Arthur with eight knights

Courtesy
—
Lamorack and Belliance

Gentleness
—
Linet mocks Gareth

13 9

Queen Guinevere Launcelot overcomes Mador

Mercy
Pelleas spares Gawaine and Ettard

Noble Acts
—
Dinadan rescues a Lady

14 10

Sir Launcelot du Lac

Prowess
—
Launcelot rescues the Queen

Quest
—
Launcelot leaves Guinevere

15 11

ASPIRATIONS
OF CHIVALRY

Queen Morgan le Fay

Marriage of Arthur and Guinevere

Malory writing in prison

4 1

Sir Mordred the Traitor

Arthur fights Accolon of Gaul

Birth of Arthur

5 2

King Arthur of England

Mordred kills Arthur

Arthur crowned king

6 3

The Lady of the Lake

Four ladies take Arthur to Avalon

Winning of Excalibur

7

LIFE AND DEATH
OF KING ARTHUR

The Malory Window:
Le Morte d'Arthur

of Launcelot and Guinevere may have been Malory's chief interest. It is like a thread that, appearing and disappearing, holds the whole library of stories together. Its human strength and weakness color even the Quest of the Holy Grail, which may be called the poetic and idyllic theme. Significantly, Launcelot comes as near the Grail's attainment as Malory could manage with any show of logic. The heart of the whole subject, the spirit of love, adventure, and of religious devotion, is formed in words which may have been written in prison and which are probably Malory's own, not a translation or a transcription.

The design for the Malory window developed through the growing recognition of important darks and lights in these legends. It resolved itself into three divisions based upon the spiritual characteristics of the tales rather than upon any effort to follow incidents in the order of their narration. These are the Life and Death of Arthur, Aspirations of Chivalry, and the Quest of the Holy Grail. Incidents and characters are used as symbols, and the three divisions are almost as clearly marked as are those of the Dante window, which is next to it.

The ornament, Celtic in character, suggests the development of natural forms as in the other three epic windows. In the bottom tier the ornament is grotesque, and suggestive of primitive beginnings aspiring toward the natural beauty of leaf (in the middle tier) and flower (in the top tier). This idea is further enriched in the small tracery pieces—the lower ones show "unnatural beasts," the middle ones show "natural beasts," while the upper tracery pieces are devoted to the Grail and its White Magic.

The shields are chosen to articulate the text with reminders of significant "men and women of Worship," Sir Launcelot, Guinevere, King Arthur, Percival's Sister, Sir Gawaine, and Sir Galahad.

Through the bottom of the window runs the inscription: "Therefore like *as May Month flowereth and flourisheth* in many gardens so in like wise *let every man of worship flourish his heart in this world, first unto God and next unto the joy of them that he promised his faith unto.*" The original text reads: Therefore lyke *as may moneth floreth and floryssheth* in many gardyns/ Soo in lyke wyse *lete euery man of worship florryss he his herte in this world/ fyrst vnto god/ and next vnto the ioye of them that he promysed his feythe vnto.* (Bk. xviii, ch. xxv, page 771, line 19)

The Bottom Tier

This tier presents the life and death of King Arthur with suggestions of black magic and violence. Dark, glowing color in the backgrounds suggests the atmosphere of early legend and war that surround the history of Arthur and the story of the sword Excalibur that is bound up with it.

"Herein may be seen noble chivalry, courtesy, humanity, friendliness, hardiness, love, cowardice, murder, hate, virtue and sin. Do after the good and leave the evil."
From Caxton's Preface

Introductory Panel 0
Syr Thomas Malory Knight
(From the short epilogue to the Morte, Bk. xxi, by Caxton)

In the lower left-hand corner, Sir Thomas Malory is shown writing Le Morte d'Arthur in Newgate Prison; symbols of the sources he used surround him: the French books, Walter de Mapes, Chrétien de Troyes, Roger de Borron, and the Scotch poet Huchown, also the printer's mark of Caxton, his publisher in 1485.

Large Figures of the Bottom Tier

Plate 14

King Arthur, right center, with spear and the true Excalibur, and Mordred the arch-traitor, left center, with sword, suggest respectively the loyalty of mediaeval tradition, the loyalty to the overlord, and treason (which was placed by Dante in the lowest hell). They correspond to the figures of Christian and Apollyon, and St. Michael and Satan in the two remaining windows. Next to the large figure of Mordred is (extreme left) a large figure of Morgan le Fay, the enchantress emblematic of evil magic, holding the false Excalibur, while to the extreme right beyond King Arthur is Nimue, the Lady of the Lake, Arthur's mystical protectress emblematic of good (white) magic, who holds the true Excalibur.

MORDRED, son of Queen Margawse of Orkney
that traytour Syr Mordred
(Bk. xxi, ch. iv, page 845, line 24)

The illegitimate son of Arthur, who finally kills him "with his sword holden in both hands and the sword pierced through helmet and brain-pan." His shield is on his left arm. There are shields of Sir Agravaine, Sir Meliagrance, and small figures represent them.

KING ARTHUR
rightwys kinge borne of all Enlond*
(Bk. i, ch. iii, iv, v, page 40, line 26)

In this bottom tier of the window, Arthur is represented as the warrior king, armed with the true Excalibur and holding the spear of his last battle. Small figures of Sir Lucan the Butler and Sir Bedivere, faithful companions of the King to the death, with their shields, and also, close to Arthur's right shoulder, shields of Launcelot and Guinevere (indented, to suggest their share in the tragedy).

* The omission of *g* is merely a printer's blunder in Caxton's text due to the position of *En* at the end of the line.

MORGAN LE FAY, Queen of Gore, wife of King Uriens
Morgan le fay . . . her fals craftes
(Bk. IV, ch. XI, page 133, line 23)

Sister and enemy of Arthur, when young she had been "put to school in a nunnery and became a great clerk of necromancy." She is described as beautiful, often given red hair. "Arthur betook the scabbard (of his sword) to Morgan and she loved another knight better than her husband or King Arthur, and she would have had her brother Arthur slain, and therefore she let make another scabbard like it by enchantment and gave sword and scabbard to her love, Sir Accolon" (Bk. II, ch. XI). Small figures flank her: Hellawes, Lady of Castle Nigramous, a sorceress who tempts Launcelot, but in vain, in the Chapel Perilous (Bk. VI, ch. XV). Annowre "was a great sorceress . . . many days she had loved King Arthur . . . brought him to her tower but the King would not have her love, then she laboured by false means to have destroyed King Arthur. King Arthur smote off her head and the Lady of the Lake hung it on her saddle bow" (Bk. IX, ch. XVI). The shields are those of Sir Accolon, Morgan le Fay, and King Arthur (indented).

LADY OF THE LAKE
lady of the lake that hyght Nyneue
(Bk. IX, ch. XVI, p. 361, line 23)

Called Nimue, she was always friendly to Arthur. She is described as "clad all in green that glistered." She shone with wonderful brightness— necklaces of gold, with opal stones and emeralds—and had a face like ivory. She holds Excalibur. The emblem of water refers to the lake of Arthurian legend, a mirage that conceals fairyland. Two small figures flank her, Merlin and Bleise: Merlin is also emblematic of friendly magic. He is usually represented as aged and bearded, and is variously described in the text as "of merveillous prowesse," of strength of body, "grete and long of stature and brown he was and lean and rough of hair," "full well-furnished of body and of members," a great gentleman. He predicted the Round Table, the love of Launcelot and Guinevere, and Arthur's death. Bleise, Merlin's master, is shown with a parchment, as he is supposed to have written down the history of Arthur's battles. He told Merlin the use of the Grail, and is shown cowled, as a hermit, the confessor of Merlin's mother and the baptizer of Merlin. The shields are those of Merlin, the Lady of the Lake, and Bleise.

Panels of the Bottom Tier

The panels begin at the lower left, following Panel 0. They read from left to right.

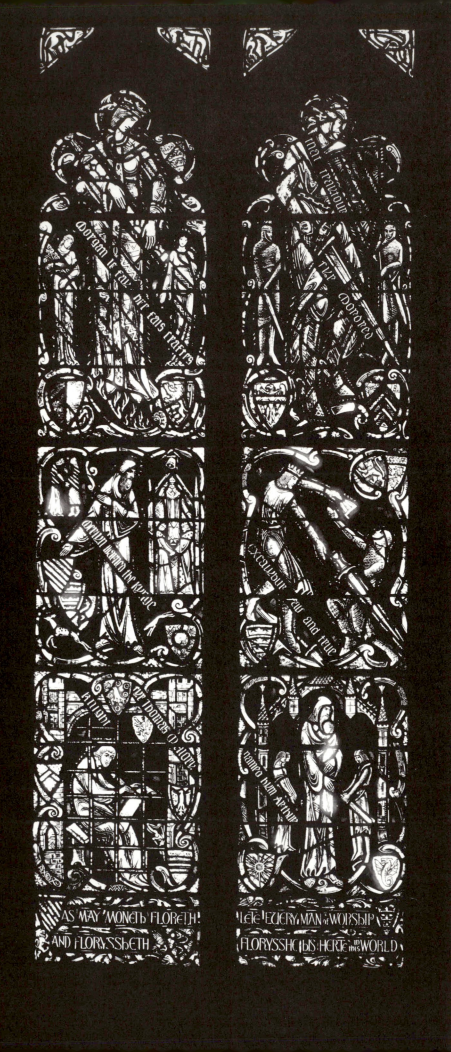

14 The Malory Window,
The Bottom Tier

1. The Birth of Arthur
named hym Arthur
(Bk. I, ch. III, p. 39, line 10)

The young child, wrapped in a cloth of gold, is delivered to Merlin, who is dressed as a poor man, by two knights and two ladies at a postern gate of the castle. "So the child was delivered unto Merlin and so he bare it forth unto Sir Ector and made an holy man to christen him, and named him Arthur" (Bk. I, ch. III). The shields are those of Uther Pendragon, Arthur's father, and Sir Ector, his half-brother.

2. Arthur is Crowned King
Arthur unto our kyng
(Bk. I, ch. VII, p. 43, line 27)

"And at the feast of Pentecost all manner of men essayed to pull at the sword that would essay, but none might prevail but Arthur, and pulled it out before all the lords and commons that were there wherefore all the commons cried at once. 'We will have Arthur unto our king.'" The shields are those of King Arthur and Sir Kay.

3. The Winning of Excalibur
How Arthur . . . gate Excalybur
(Bk. I, ch. XXV, p. 7, line 5)

"So Sir Arthur and Merlin alit and tied their horses to two trees and so they went into the ship, and when they came to the sword that the hand held, Sir Arthur took it with him and the arm and the hand went under the water" (Bk. I, ch. XXV). Arms of the Lady of the Lake and of Merlin.

4. The Marriage of Arthur and Guinevere
Merlyn warned the Kynge
(Bk. III, ch. I, p. 100, line 25)

This is designed to include Merlin's prophecy of Launcelot the lover, suggested also by the white hart and the brachet. "Then was high feast made ready, and the King was wedded at Camelot unto the Dame Guenevere . . . with great solemnity" (Bk. III, ch. V). The shields are those of Launcelot and Guinevere, separated by those of Arthur, and of King Leodegrance, her father.

5. The Fight between King Arthur and Accolon of Gaul
Excalibur fals and true (Bk. IV, ch. X)

This battle is significant of the power of Excalibur, of the Black Magic of Morgan le Fay, and of the White Magic of Nimue (Bk. IV, ch. IX–X). "When the Damosel of the Lake beheld Arthur, how full of prowess his body was, and the false treason that was wrought for him to have him slain, she had great pity . . . and at the next stroke Sir Accolon struck him such a stroke that by the damsel's enchantment Excalibur fell out of Accolon's hand. . . . And therewithal Sir Arthur lightly lept to it, and gat it in his hand . . . and pulled the scabbard from him and threw it from him. . . . And . . . Sir Arthur rushed on him with all his might and pulled him to earth, and then rushed off his helm." The King spares him to ask where he got Excalibur, and is told that it was from Morgan le Fay, King Arthur's sister. Shields of Accolon and Arthur (in action), and of Morgan le Fay and Nimue.

6. Mordred and Arthur Fight to the Death
Le Morte d'Arthur

"Then was King Arthur ware where Sir Mordred leaned upon his sword among a great heap of dead men. Now give me my spear, said King Arthur to Sir Lucan, for yonder I have spied the traitor that all this woe hath wrought. . . . And when Sir Mordred felt that he had his death wound he thrust himself with the might he had up to the bur of King Arthur's spear . . . and therewithal Sir Mordred fell stark dead to the earth and the noble Arthur fell in a swoon to the earth" (Bk. XXI, ch. IV). Shields of Sir Lucan and Sir Bedivere.

7. Excalibur is Returned to the Lake
To Auylyon to hele me of my greuous wounds
(Bk. XXI, ch. V, p. 850, lines 2–3)

The Dark Barge of King Arthur with the four veiled Queens (symbolic of Arthur's death). "Fast by the bank hoved a little barge with many fair ladies in it and all they had black hoods, and they all wept and shrieked when they saw King Arthur . . . there received him three queens with great mourning (the fourth queen being the Lady of the Lake) . . . in one of their laps King Arthur laid his head. . . . And then they rowed from the land." In the background may be seen Excalibur, returned to the mere, and caught and brandished by the arm in white samite. The shields are those of the Queen of Northgalis, the Queen of Orkney, Morgan le Fay Queen of Gore, and the Lady of the Lake.

Large Figures of the Middle Tier

The Middle Tier celebrates the aspirations of Chivalry, with central symbols of the Fellowship of the Round Table and of Romantic Love as it was revealed by Malory in the championships of the Tournament. King Arthur dominates the Round Table as Queen Guinevere dominates the Joust between Sir Mador and Sir Launcelot (disguised).

KING ARTHUR
all knyȝtes maye lerne to be a knyghte of hym
(Bk. X, ch. LXIII, p. 542, line 26)

Standing for kingship and loyalty, Arthur is the commanding figure of this tier and completes the symbol of the Round Table. He is flanked by the eight knights who are also shown below in the panels of the Chivalric Virtues (the sacramental quality of true brotherhood). The eight knights are: Sir Launcelot, Sir Gareth, Sir Dinadan, Sir Palamedes, Sir Tristram, Sir Lamorack, Sir Pelleas, Sir Gawaine. Galahad seated in the Siege Perilous, in front of the King, completes the group of nine to recall the "Nine Kings that served Arthur at Table." Above, close to Arthur's shoulder are shields of Launcelot and Guinevere (overlapped).

QUEEN GUINEVERE
quene Gueneuer . . . hir beaulte & hir noblesse
(Bk. XXI, ch. IX, p. 857, line 35)

She is described as "clothed in white cloth of gold tissue" (Bk. XX, ch. XIV). "While she lived she was a good lover, therefore she had a good end" (Bk. XVIII, ch. XXV).

In front of Guinevere is a symbol of the field of honor, a reminder of the fight for the Queen when a strange knight on a white horse (Launcelot) bested her traducer Sir Mador. The arms of Guinevere are worn by heralds, and on the trumpets are the arms of Launcelot and Arthur. Sir Mador carries his own shield (in the Tournament) and Launcelot a white shield.

SIR LAUNCELOT (extreme right)
Syr Launcelot du lake
(Bk. VI, ch. I, p. 183, title above chapter)

"And thou were the courteoust knight that ever bare shield. And thou were the truest friend to thy lover that ever bestrad horse. . . . And thou were the kindest man that ever struck with sword. . . . And thou were the meekest man and the gentlest that ever ate in hall among Ladies. And thou were the sternest knight to thy mortal foe that ever put spear in the rest." Words of Sir Ector over the body of Sir Launcelot (Bk. XXI, ch. XIII). Small figures of Launcelot as a Monk (right) and of Guinevere as a Nun (left), both bearing blank scrolls for forgiveness. Sir Launcelot bears the shield of Le Chevalier Mal Fet, and the red sleeve of Elaine le Blank on his helm. Shields (above) of King Ban, his supposed father, and of Sir Ector de Maris, his half brother; below are those of Guinevere and Launcelot.

SIR TRISTRAM (extreme left)
Syr Tristram de lyones
(Bk. IX, ch. XIX, p. 367, line 20)

Tristram stands for faithful love and friendship. In white armor, he is shown with the shield of Morgan le Fay. "Of goodly harping he beareth the prize in the world" (Bk. IX, ch. XVIII). His harp appears in the background. The small figures are: Sir Alisander le Orphelm (Bk. X, ch. XXXVI), wearing his father's bloody doublet and blood-stained shirt "to his death day" in memory of his revenge; and Sir Pelleas, "One of the best knights in the world," with the circlet he gave Ettard, that he won at the jousts. The shields are those of Sir Tristram, Sir Alisander, Sir Pelleas, and La Beale Isoud (La Belle Iseult).

Panels of the Middle Tier

Incidents from the adventures of the "most famous" knights are chosen here to represent the eight virtues that Caxton noted in his preface: Friendship, Gentleness, Noble Acts, Quest, Faithfulness, Courtesy, Mercy, Prowess. Galahad, who appears in the Siege Perilous in the Round Table, is also represented by implication in the small figures of the "Quest" panel.

8. *Frendshyp.* Tristram Accords with Launcelot

"Fair knight, he said, my name is Launcelot du Lac. Alas, said Sir Tristram, what have I done, for ye are the man in the world that I love most. Fair knight, said Sir Launcelot, tell me your name. Truly, said he, my name is Sir Tristram de Liones. O Jesu, said Sir Launcelot, what adventure is befallen me! And therewith Sir Launcelot kneeled down and yielded him up his sword. And therewithal Sir Tristram kneeled down and yielded him up his sword. And so either gave other the degree" (Bk. X, ch. V). "And so at the last, by both their assents, they were made better friends and sworn brethren for ever, and no man can judge the better knight" (Bk. X, ch. XVI). The shields are those of Launcelot and Tristram.

9. *Veray gentylnesse.*

Beaumains (Gareth) is mocked by the damosel Linet, after he has overcome the Red Knight, and bears it patiently. "But always the damosel spake many foul words unto Beaumains . . . and ever she chided him in the foulest manner . . . and he suffered it patiently. 'Away kitchen knave, out of the window, for the smell of thy bawdy clothes grieveth me . . . Fie upon thee, false kitchen page.' Damosel, said Beaumains, ye are uncourteous so to rebuke me as ye do—but first I let you wit that I will not depart from you" (Bk. VII, ch. IX, X, XI). The Black and Red shields are those of the knights whom Gareth overthrew and his own shield.

10. *Noble actes.* Dinadan Rescues a Lady

"So as Dinadan rode by a well he found a lady making great dole. . . . Sir knight, said the lady, I am the wofullest lady of the world, for within these five days here came . . . Sir Breuse Sance Pitie, and he slew mine own brother, and hath kept me at his will . . . I require you of knighthood to avenge me. . . . Let him come, said Sir Dinadan . . . came Sir Breuse, and he was wood wroth. So they hurtled together as thunder and either smote other passing sore, but Sir Dinadan put him through the shoulder a grievous wound, and or ever Sir Dinadan might turn him Sir Breuse was gone and fled. Then the lady prayed him to bring her to a castle . . . and so Sir Dinadan brought her there and she was welcome . . . and Sir Dinadan rode his way" (Bk. IX, ch. XLI). The shields are those of Sir Dinadan and Sir Breuse Sance Pitie.

11. *Quest*. Launcelot's Farewell to Queen Guinevere in the Quest of the Grail (Bk. XIII, ch. VIII)

"When Sir Launcelot missed the Queen, he went into her chamber and when she saw him cried aloud, 'Ye have put me to the death for to leave thus, my lord.'" Palamedes and the Questing Beast (at the bottom of the panel), a symbol of all quests, has a head like a serpent, a body like a leopard (Bk. IX, ch. XIII). There are also figures of mounted knights on the Quest. The shields are those of Launcelot and Palamedes.

12. *Feythfulnesse*. Tristram and Isoud drink the Love Drink

"And . . . then Sir Tristram took the flacket in his hand and said, Madam Isoud, here is the best drink that ever ye drank, that Dame Bragwaine your maiden, and Gouvernail my servant, have kept for themselves. Then they laughed and made good cheer, and either drank to other freely and they thought never drink that ever they drank to other was so sweet nor so good. But by that their drink was in their bodies, they loved either other so well that never their love departed for weal neither for woe." The shields are those of Tristram and Isoud.

13. *Curtosye*. The Courteous Fight between Sir Lamorack and Sir Belliance le Orgulus

In a quarrel over a lady, Lamorack has slain Sir Frol, brother to Sir Belliance, who promptly arms himself and, first on horseback then on foot, fights Lamorack to revenge his brother's death. They find out each other's identity, but Belliance forces Lamorack to continue fighting. "At the last Belliance withdrew him aback and set him down softly on a little hill, for he was so faint from bleeding that he might not stand. Then Sir Lamorak threw his shield upon his back, and asked him what cheer. Well, said Belliance. Ah, sir, yet shall I show you favour in your mal-ease. Ah, knight Sir Belliance, said Sir Lamorak, thou art a fool; for and I had had thee at such advantage as thou hast done me, I should slay thee, but thy gentleness is so good and so large that I must needs forgive thee mine evil will. And then

Sir Lamorak kneeled down and unlaced first his umberere, and then his own, and then either kissed other with weeping tears" (Bk. VIII, ch. XLI). The shields are those of Lamorack and Belliance.

14. *Mercy*. Sir Pelleas Spares Gawaine and the Lady Ettard

"And then he yede to the third pavilion and found Sir Gawaine lying in bed with his lady, Ettard, and either clipping other in arms, and when he saw that his heart wellnight brast for sorrow . . . and pulled out his sword naked in his hand, and went to them thereas they lay, and yet he thought it were shame to slay them sleeping, and laid the naked sword overthwart both their throats, and so took his horse and rode his way" (Bk. IV, ch. XXII). The shields are those of Pelleas and Gawaine (indented).

15. *Prowesse*. Sir Launcelot Rescues the Queen

After a desperate battle in which he kills the faithful Gareth, Sir Launcelot rescues the Queen from being burned at the stake (Bk. XX, ch. VIII). "Then when Sir Launcelot had thus done and slain and put to flight all that would withstand him, then he rode straight unto Dame Guinevere and made a kirtle and a gown to be cast upon her . . . and then he made her to set behind him." At the upper left is his castle to which they escaped, and at upper left the flames at the stake. The shields are those of Gareth (indented) and Launcelot.

Large Figures of the Top Tier

This tier is devoted to the search for the Grail. Here worldly adventure yields to the quest of the spirit. The figures of the four "great companions," Bors, Percival, Percival's Sister, and Galahad, are treated as mediaeval symbols of spiritual aspiration. They are mounted and the three knights are armed. Percival's Sister holds a cross instead of the sword, to symbolize the spiritual victory over death that marks her self-sacrifice.

A large inscription runs beneath the mounted figures, words spoken by Christ during the vision of the Grail at Carbonek. White and red are the colors of the Grail, white for the earth lit by visions not of this world, red for celestial love. These colors accordingly dominate in the upper section.

> *my knyghtes//and//my seruauntes// and my true*
> *children whiche ben//come//oute of dedely lyf//*
> *into spyrytual lyf//I wyl now no longer hyde*
> *me from yow/*   (Bk. XVII, ch. XX, p. 719, line 20)

BORS.
syre Bors
(Bk. XVI, ch. XV, p. 685, line 19)

The eldest of the three knights, he symbolizes the active life in contrast with Percival. Simple human loyalty was the keynote of his character. He is dressed in his heraldic colors, with touches of scarlet to suggest his undergarment of penitence. "Instead of a shirt and a sign of chastisement ye shall wear a garment, . . . a scarlet coat that should be instead of his shirt till he had fulfilled the San Grael" (Bk. XVI, ch. VII).

PERCIVAL.
Syr Percyual
(Bk. XIV, ch. VI, p. 649, lines 20–22)

Symbol of contemplative knighthood, Percival's costume combines knightly trappings and the somber (tan-violet) robe of a monk, significant of his religious zeal and of his later life as a monk.

PERCIVAL'S SISTER.
blessid mayden
(Bk. XVII, ch. VII, p. 700, line 13)

Symbol of sacrifice, this is the gentlest and most appealing of all Malory's characters. She offers a gracious contrast to the prevailing violence of these tales. Her story of renunciation and dedication has a mystical significance above the valorous deeds of her companions. Her name is never given, but she was a daughter of King Pellinore. She is described as having short yellow hair. "When I wist that this adventure was ordained me I clipped off my hair" (Bk. XVII, ch. VII). She wears the pure red of love and martyrdom and carries the red cross.

GALAHAD.
syr Galahad
(Bk. XVI, ch. XVII, p. 688, line 16)

Symbol of the pure in heart, he is described as clad in the flame-red of charity; his armor "shone like a star of fire."

Panels of the Top Tier

The two panels below each figure relate, in adventures of the spirit as well as of earth, the progress of each toward perfection. Since the direction of this tier is vertical, the panels should be read from the bottom up.

16. Temptation of Bors
I am greuously escaped
(Bk. XVI, ch. XII, p. 681, line 11)

Bors is tempted by a devil, in the guise of a beautiful woman. She goes up to a high battlement and tells him that she and her twelve gentlewomen will throw themselves off the tower if she cannot have his love. ". . . and with that they fell adown all at once into the earth. And when he saw that, he was all abashed, . . . With that he blessed his body and his visage. And anon he heard a great noise and a great cry as though all the fiends of hell had been about him; and therewith he saw neither tower, nor lady, nor gentlewomen, . . . Then held he up both his hands to the heaven, and said: Fair Father God, I am grievously escaped; and then he took his arms and his horse and rode on his way" (Bk. xvi, ch. xii). Sir Bors is dressed in doublet and robe lined with ermine, significant of Luxury. The shield is that of Sir Bors.

17. Bors to the Rescue
Syr knyghte lete your hand of that mayden
(Bk. xvi, ch. x)

Bors rescues the maid instead of his brother. He fights with the Black Knight and overcomes him. "Then dressed he him unto the knight the which had the gentlewoman, and then he cried, Sir knight let your hand off that maiden, or ye be but dead. And then he set down the maiden, and was armed at all pieces save he lacked his spear. Then he dressed his shield, and drew out his sword, and Bors smote him so hard that it went through his shield and habergeon on the left shoulder. And through great strength he beat him down to the earth and at the pulling out of Bors' spear there he swooned. Then Bors came to the maid . . . and took the horse of the wounded knight and set the gentlewoman upon him." To protect purity, a spiritual quality, is a greater thing than to protect life, a material quality. Lionel his brother, naked and bleeding, his hands bound, is on a horse between two knights. Shield of Sir Bors and that of the Black Knight under Bors' spear signifying defeat.

18. Percival Tempted by a Fiend
commaunded hymself vnto god
(Bk. xiv, ch. vi, p. 648, line 24)

The adventure on the great horse which was "blacker than any bear." "And when Sir Percival came nigh the brim, and saw the water so boistrous, he doubted to overpass it. And then he made the sign of the cross in his forehead. When the fiend felt him so charged, he shook off Sir Percival, and he went into the water crying and roaring, making great sorrow, and it seemed unto him that the water brent. Then Sir Percival perceived it was the fiend the which would have brought him unto his perdition. Then he commended himself unto God, and prayed Our Lord to keep him from all such temptations; and so he prayed all that night" (Bk. xiv, ch. v and vi). The shield is Sir Percival's.

19. Percival Tempted by a Lady
ne let me not be shamed
(Bk. xiv, ch. x, p. 654, line 16)

Percival resists temptation through the Cross in the pommel of his sword (Bk. xiv, ch. ix). "And anon she (fair lady) was unclothed . . . and by adventure and grace he saw his sword . . . in whose pommel was a red cross . . .

and bethought him on his knighthood . . . made the sign of the cross on his forehead, and therewith the pavilion turned up-so-down . . . changed into a smoke . . . and then he was adread and cried loudly: Fair sweet Father, Jesus Christ, ne let me not be shamed." The shield is Percival's.

20, 21. The Sacrifice of Percival's Sister
am come to the dethe//for to make yow hole
(Bk. XVII, ch. XI, p. 706, line 4)

In the lower panel is shown the Custom of the Castle, where a sick lady may be healed only by the blood of a pure virgin. "And Sir Percival's Sister bade bring forth the sick lady. So she was, the which was evil at ease. Then said she: Who shall let me blood? So one came forth and let her blood and she bled so much that the dish was full. Then she lift up her hand and blessed her; and then she said to the Lady: Madam I am come to the death for to make you whole, for God's love pray for me. With that she fell into a swoon."

The passage is continued in the upper panel where Percival's Sister, having saved the lady's life, dies. "Then Galahad and his two fellows start up to her, and lift her up and staunched her, but she had bled so much that she might not live. Then she said when she was awaked: Fair brother Percival, I die for the healing of this lady, so I require you that ye bury me not in this country, but as soon as I am dead put me in a boat at the next haven, and let me go as adventure will lead me; and as soon as ye three will come to the City of Sarras, there to enchieve the Holy Grail, ye shall find me under a tower arrived and there bury me in the spiritual place; for I say you so much, there Galahad shall be buried, and ye also in the same place. . . . Then asked she her Saviour; and as soon as she had received it the soul departed from the body." Note the small symbol of Castle and Queen drooping (in the lower panel, 20) and erect (in the panel above, 21) to balance each figure of Percival's Sister.

22. Galahad's Knighting by Sir Launcelot
god make hym a good man
(Bk. XIII, ch. I, p. 613, line 22)

"On the morn at the hour of prime, at Galahad's desire, he made him knight and said: God make him a good man." The shields are those of Sir Launcelot and Sir Galahad.

23. Galahad in the Siege Perilous and the Appearance of the Grail
the holy graile
(Bk. XIII, ch. VII, p. 620, line 12)

". . . anon they heard cracking and crying of thunder that them thought the place should all to-drive. In the midst of this blast entered a sunbeam more clearer by seven times than ever they saw day, and all they were alighted by the grace of the Holy Ghost. . . . then there entered into the hall the Holy Grail covered with white samite, but there was none might see it, nor who bare it. And there was all the hall fulfilled with good odours . . . and when the Holy Grail had been borne through the hall, then the holy vessel departed suddenly."

The Tracery of the Top Tier

The Tracery symbolizes the achievement of the Grail and the mediaeval conception of Christ as it is revealed in the whitest of white magic. The dominant piece is devoted to The Grail itself—the Christ of the vision of Carbonek: "a man come out of the Holy Vessel that had all the signs of the passion of Jesu Christ, bleeding all openly . . . and said, My Knights and my servants etc." Here is symbolized the Mediaeval Christ as distinct from the visions offered by the other Epics. The four Angels of the Passion, St. Joseph of Arimathea, the Twelve Holy Doves, stars and clouds of Heavenly Vision complete the design.

24. The development of the theme in the twelve books of the great Puritan epic is divided in this window into the Fall of the Angels (bottom tier), the Fall of Man (middle tier), and Man's Redemption (top tier). The top panel farthest right in the bottom and middle tiers is the crucial link in the epic's progress from one phase to the next. The inscription that serves as a theme for the entire composition runs across the band below the bottom tier of panels:

SOUTHEAST BAY:
MILTON,
PARADISE LOST (24)

> *Celestial light*
> *Shine inward, that I may see and tell*
> *Of things invisible to mortal sight.**
>
> (Bk. III, line 51)

The inscription is enriched by the coat of arms of Milton's family and by seven small figures with books to symbolize the probable sources of the ideas which the poem develops and embellishes: Moses; The Gospel of John; Enoch, for the Jewish spirit of Zohar; the Kabbalah; St. Paul; St. Augustine; Robert Flood, a mystic of Milton's time.

The Bottom Tier

The Introductory Panel 0
That . . . I may . . . Justifie the wayes of God to men.
(Bk. I, lines 24–26)

The blind Milton is dictating to his daughter while at the upper right stands a small figure of Satan, defiant, with bat-like wings and clad in armor.

Plate 15

* The quotations used for the inscriptions are taken from the original text, the second edition of Paradise Lost, revised by the author and published in 1674.

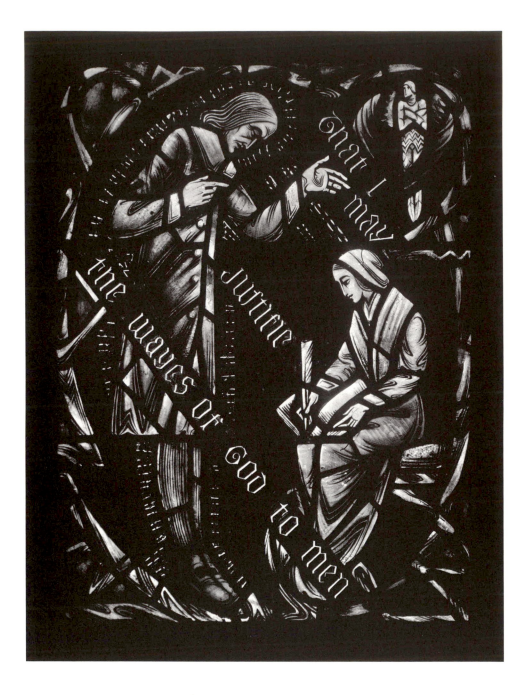

15 The Milton Window,
Introductory Panel

The bottom tier is devoted to the combat between the heavenly host and the rebellious angels led by Satan, his plan of revenge, after the fall, leading to his entering the new-formed earth.

Large Figures of the Bottom Tier

Four large figures occupy the upper parts of the lancets (1–3; 11):

1. The Messiah
Eternal wrauth
Burnt after them to the bottomless pit.
(Bk. VI, line 865)

The Messiah in His chariot, clothed in armor, with the eagle of victory in His right hand and His bow and quiver filled with thunders, drives the hosts of evil before Him. The chariot, "flashing thick flames, wheel within wheel indrawn," is conveyed by four Cherubim, each with four faces, their bodies and wings all set with eyes (Bk. VI, line 750).

2, 3. Michael and Satan
Michael of Celestial Armies Prince (Bk. VI, line 44).
Satan Antagonist of Heaven's King (Bk. X, line 386).

Michael and Satan occupy the two central lancets. These symbolize in a general way the combat between good and evil. Satan's sword has been cut in two by Michael's and he wears armor of adamant and gold, as is worn by the angels, but it has lost much of its former brilliance. In this combat Satan, wounded, "first knew pain and writhed him to and fro, convolved, so sore the griding sword with discontinuous wound pass'd through him" (Bk. VI, lines 327-30). This stirring phase of the battle was recounted to Adam by Raphael. In the second phase of the combat Satan had created an infernal artillery which threw the angels into confusion so that God sent His Son, on the third day, to end the combat. The Satanic host were driven to the wall of Heaven. It opened and they leaped down into the place of punishment in the deep. Below the figure of Satan a small cannon is emblematic of the temporary advantage of the Satanic hosts.

Satan is shown again at the top of the lancet farthest right (11), but in connection with a later phase of the epic. We should look first at the rest of the panels in this tier, beginning with those directly under the three large figures just described. These represent Angelic Combats and symbolize the defeat of Satan's host.

Panels of the Bottom Tier

4. Gabriel defeats Moloch
The figures represent wisdom overcoming brute force.

5. Raphael defeats Asmadai

78

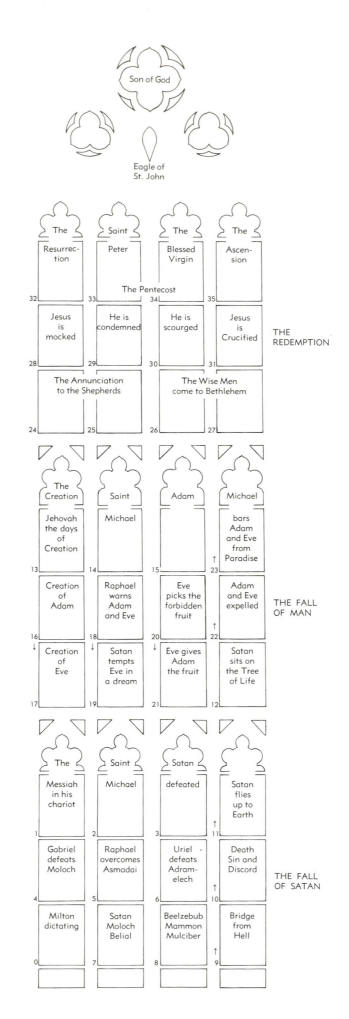

Son of God

Eagle of
St. John

The Resurrection	Saint Peter	The Blessed Virgin	The Ascension

The Pentecost

| 32 | 33 | 34 | 35 |

Jesus is mocked	He is condemned	He is scourged	Jesus is Crucified

THE REDEMPTION

| 28 | 29 | 30 | 31 |

The Annunciation to the Shepherds		The Wise Men come to Bethlehem	

| 24 | 25 | 26 | 27 |

The Creation	Saint	Adam	Michael
Jehovah the days of Creation	Michael		bars Adam and Eve from Paradise

| 13 | 14 | 15 | 23 |

Creation of Adam	Raphael warns Adam and Eve	Eve picks the forbidden fruit	Adam and Eve expelled

THE FALL OF MAN

| 16 | 18 | 20 | 22 |

Creation of Eve	Satan tempts Eve in a dream	Eve gives Adam the fruit	Satan sits on the Tree of Life

| 17 | 19 | 21 | 12 |

The	Saint	Satan	
Messiah in his chariot	Michael	defeated	Satan flies up to Earth

| 1 | 2 | 3 | 11 |

Gabriel defeats Moloch	Raphael overcomes Asmadai	Uriel defeats Adramelech	Death Sin and Discord

THE FALL OF SATAN

| 4 | 5 | 6 | 10 |

Milton dictating	Satan Moloch Belial	Beelzebub Mammon Mulciber	Bridge from Hell

| 0 | 7 | 8 | 9 |

The Milton Window:
Paradise Lost

6. Uriel defeats Adramelech

Uriel is shown descending on a sunbeam and overcoming Adramelech ("and I saw an angel standing in the sun" Rev. 19:17). The scene illustrates the victory of Heavenly knowledge.

7, 8. Satan in Hell
Better to reign in Hell, than serve in Heav'n.
(Bk. I, line 263)

The two central panels below show on the left Satan flanked on his right by Moloch, "the strongest and the fiercest Spirit/ That fought in Heav'n" (II. 45), and on his left by Belial, "A fairer person lost not Heav'n .../But all was false and hollow" (II. 110). To the right is Beelzebub, next after Satan in the hierarchy of Hell. Beside him, Mammon clutches a bag of coins, and Mulciber (I. 740) holds his architect's compass. The Palace of Pandemonium, which he designed, appears as a pagan temple with pillars above and behind all six figures. The inscription quotes Satan's words.

The remaining panels (9, 10, 11) symbolize Satan's plan of revenge and his ascent to Earth.

9. The Bridge to Earth
A Bridge . . . from Hell . . . (to) this frail world.
(Bk. II, line 1026)

Hell's Gates and the Bridge built to earth are lit with the flames of the evil spirits.

10. Death, Sin, Discord
Sin and Death . . . following in his track
(Bk. II, line 1024)

Death, Sin, and Discord are seen on their way to earth. Sin is shown as a monster with the figure of a "woman to the waist, and fair,/ But ended foul in many a scaly fould/ Voluminous and vast, a Serpent arm'd/ With mortal sting" (Bk. II, lines 650-53). She is preceded by "Death, son of Satan" (Bk. II, line 629). Following the two comes Discord, the first daughter of Sin.

11. Satan Flanked by Sin and Death
Long is the way and hard, that out of Hell
Leads up to light.
(Bk. II, line 423)

This top panel of the fourth lancet shows Sin and Death, "The other shape/ If shape it might be call'd that shape had none . . . black it stood as Night,/ Fierce as ten Furies, terrible as Hell, And shook a dreadful Dart;/ what seem'd his head/ The likeness of a Kingly Crown had on." They are on either side of Satan, winged as he flies up to Earth.

In the small tracery pieces at the top of the bottom tier are simple shapes to suggest "Chaos and the spirits of the Nethermost Abyss." They comprise King Chaos and his consort, Night; Orcus and Ades; and four qualities associated with the power of evil: Rumor, Chance, Tumult, and Confusion.

The Middle Tier

Following the revolt of the Angels and their fall as shown in the bottom tier, the middle section of the window is emblematic of the Creation, Man's Temptation in the Garden of Eden, his Fall, and the Promise of Redemption. Here are shown the success of Satan's revenge and his final defeat as symbolized by the revelation of the Redemption made by Michael to Adam.

Large Figures of the Middle Tier

13. The Creation
His brooding wings the spirit of God outspread.
(Bk. VII, line 235)

Here at the extreme left is the Creation, symbolized by the figure of Jehovah, borne on the wings of cherubim and surrounded by the symbols of the six days of creation as He holds the golden compass with which He marked the circumference of the world out of Chaos. The six symbols illustrate the Creation of Light, the Land and Sea, the Growing Things, the Heavenly Bodies—Sun, Moon, and Stars—the Birds, Fishes, and finally Man.

14, 15. The Revelation and the Promise
So both ascend/ In the Visions of God.
(Bk. XI, line 376)

In the central panels Michael and Adam illustrate the Revelation that Michael made to Adam and the Promise of Redemption. Surrounding each of the two figures are scenes that symbolize the great prophecy of promise, as found in the Old Testament and fulfilled in the New Testament (Bk. XI, lines 430 ff). The scene of Cain killing Abel and the Lazar House show the effects of Adam's transgression on his descendants; the Deluge exhibits mortality and loss but also that God keeps his covenant with Noah; Abraham, Moses, and David show the promise of the Messiah becoming more and more definite. The New Testament cycle shows the fulfillment of the promise; the Nativity of Christ, His Crucifixion, the Resurrection, His Appearance at the Supper at Emmaus, the Last Judgment, and the Messiah enthroned. Michael is shown at the top of the right-hand lancet but, as in the bottom tier, we should save this panel until last since it is the bridge that crosses to the top tier.

Panels of the Middle Tier

These illustrate in greater detail the events that are summed up in the large figures.

12. Satan's Arrival on Earth
. . . within him Hell| He brings.
(Bk. iv, line 20)

At the lower right, above the ascent of Satan illustrated in the lowest tier, is his arrival on Earth where, in the form of a cormorant, he sits on the Tree of Life. Below him are the toad and snake, which were two of his disguises, and around are the four rivers that watered the earthly paradise.

16. The Creation of Adam
Adam, rise| First man.
(Bk. vii, line 297)

17. The Creation of Eve from Adam's Rib
Woman is her name.
(Bk. viii, line 495)

18. Raphael Warns Adam and Eve
To thy obedience, therein stand.
(Bk. v, line 522)

Raphael warns Adam and Eve as they receive him in their bower. Eve is shown quite appropriately as waiting on Raphael and Adam.

19. Satan Tempts Eve
Artificer of Fraud
(Bk. iv, line 121)

As Eve sleeps in her bower, Satan has taken the form of a toad and whispers in her ear. A moonbeam, symbol of the angel Ithuriel (Search of God), touches him. Above are the celestial golden scales, weighed down on one side and giving the sign at which Satan took his flight.

20. The Temptation of Eve
. . . the Tree
Of prohibition, root of all our woe.
(Bk. ix, line 644)

Eve plucks the fruit of the Tree of Knowledge as the Serpent tempts her by telling of its virtues.

21. Adam Tempted by Eve
Shee gave him of that fair enticing fruit.
(Bk. ix, line 996)

Eve gives Adam the forbidden fruit. In one hand she holds a bough from the Tree, covered with fruit and leaves. A garland of roses falls from Adam's hand, to signify the end of the blissful paradise.

22. Adam and Eve Expelled from Paradise
dust thou art and shalt to dust return.
(Bk. x, line 208)

Adam and Eve are girded with fig leaves; their heads are bowed in guilt and shame, while in front of them is shown the flaming sword set to prohibit their return.

23. Adam and Eve Go out into the World
. . . Shalt possess
A paradise within thee,/ happier far.
(Bk. xii, line 585)

In the lancet above, Michael with flaming sword bars the entrance to Paradise while Adam and Eve, clothed in the skins of beasts, stand erect as they go out into the world.

Above the four lancets of the middle tier eight small pieces in the tracery are designed to express the labors of four seasons—one of Milton's favorite symbols of the changing beauty of the earth.

The Top Tier

After the fall of man, as shown in the middle tier of the window, follows his redemption according to the vision that Michael showed to Adam. Milton's majestic theme—the intervention of Omnipotence itself to prevent the destruction of mankind by the united powers of Hell—is celebrated in glorious colors in which blue, the heavenly color, predominates. Through the bottom row of panels runs an inscription in vertical lines:

but now I see
His day in whom
all Nations shall be
blest.
(Bk. xii, line 276)

The panels read horizontally from left to right. The first two show the Annunciation of the glad tidings to the Shepherds (24) by Angels (25). Panels 26–27 show the Wise Men coming to Bethlehem, and the Holy Family.

In the row next above are the scenes that illustrate Christ's sufferings and condemnation as described by the poet:

28. Jesus is mocked by His enemies
For this He shall live hated.

29: He is condemned by the Sanhedrin for blasphemy
be blasphemed

30. Jesus is scourged
Seised . . . judged

31. He is crucified between the two thieves
And to death condemned.
(Bk. xii, lines 411–12)

The large figures at the tops of the lancets are: Christ at the Resurrection (32). In the lower corners of the panel and turned away from the figure of Christ are Sin and Satan, each in the form of a serpent. Directly below Christ's feet lies Death, as a symbol of His victory. Next to Christ stands St. Peter (33), flanked by the other Apostles. On his head, as on theirs, are the flames of the Spirit of God—the Pentecost. Next to him stands the Blessed Virgin (34), flanked likewise by Apostles who also have above their heads the fire of the Pentecost. In the scene of the Ascension (35) the Apostles kneel on either side of Christ.

Across the base of all four panels runs the inscription:

His spirit within them and the Law of Faith
Working through Love upon their hearts
all write to guide them in all truth.
(Bk. xii, line 488)

In the tracery above are cherubim, seraphim, stars, comets, and flames. In the rose is the Son of God. Just below Him appears the Eagle, symbol of St. John the Evangelist, from whose Gospel Milton derived his inspiration. The inscription in the rose reads:

Hail, Son of God, Savior of Men.
(Bk. iii, line 412)

25. Like Milton's Paradise Lost, John Bunyan's masterpiece takes its inspiration from the Bible. Written in prison, where Bunyan had already served twelve years as a dissenting preacher who refused to be silent at the Restoration, the narrative takes the familiar and beloved form of a journey by a common man into unknown country. His name is Christian and he is in search of his spiritual inheritance. Through each tier runs a continuous series of panels descriptive of the journey's encounters and adventures, with the large figures above portraying the protagonists in each tier.

SOUTH BAY.
BUNYAN,
PILGRIM'S PROGRESS (25)

Across the base of the whole window is inscribed Christian's purpose, with its quotation from 1 Peter 1:4:

I seek an inheritance incorruptible, undefiled, and that
*fadeth not away; and it is laid up in heaven.**
(Page 11, lines 22, 23)

* The source of the quotations and inscriptions may be found in Bunyan, *The Pilgrim's Progress*, edited by James Blanton Wharey, 2nd ed., revised by Roger Sharrock. Oxford Clarendon Press, 1960.

84

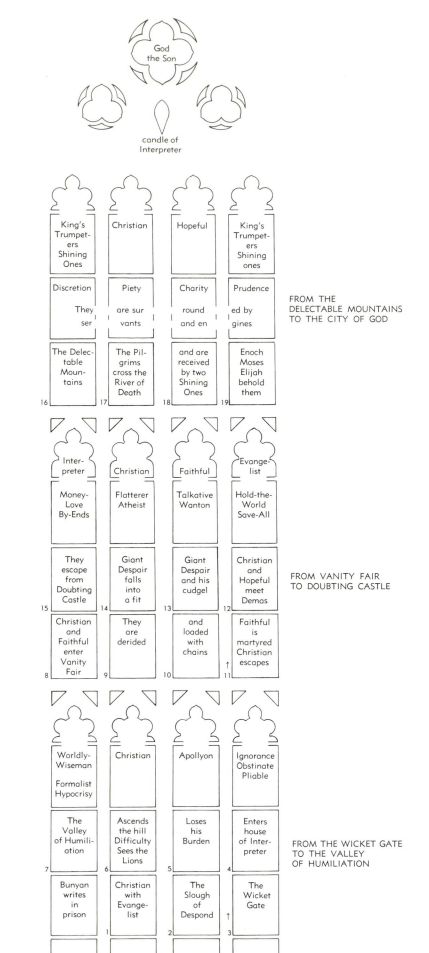

God
the Son

candle of
Interpreter

King's Trumpet-ers Shining Ones	Christian	Hopeful	King's Trumpet-ers Shining ones
Discretion — They — ser	Piety — are sur — vants	Charity — round — and en	Prudence — ed by — gines
The Delec-table Moun-tains	The Pil-grims cross the River of Death	and are received by two Shining Ones	Enoch Moses Elijah behold them
16	17	18	19

FROM THE
DELECTABLE MOUNTAINS
TO THE CITY OF GOD

Inter-preter	Christian	Faithful	Evange-list
Money-Love By-Ends	Flatterer Atheist	Talkative Wanton	Hold-the-World Save-All
They escape from Doubting Castle	Giant Despair falls into a fit	Giant Despair and his cudgel	Christian and Hopeful meet Demas
Christian and Faithful enter Vanity Fair	They are derided	and loaded with chains	Faithful is martyred Christian escapes
15 8	14 9	13 10	12 11

FROM VANITY FAIR
TO DOUBTING CASTLE

Worldly-Wiseman Formalist Hypocrisy	Christian	Apollyon	Ignorance Obstinate Pliable
The Valley of Humili-ation	Ascends the hill Difficulty Sees the Lions	Loses his Burden	Enters house of Inter-preter
Bunyan writes in prison	Christian with Evange-list	The Slough of Despond	The Wicket Gate
7	6 1	5 2	4 3

The Bunyan Window:
Pilgrim's Progress

FROM THE WICKET GATE
TO THE VALLEY
OF HUMILIATION

The panels are to be read from the extreme lower left horizontally to the right, and the following row the reverse way.

Bottom Tier

The panel at the lower left represents Bunyan in Prison dreaming and writing *Pilgrim's Progress*. He is surrounded by figures of the Evangelists and Prophets, and by that of John Fox who wrote the *Book of Martyrs*.

Plate 16

> *Writing of the Way and Race of Saints in this Our Gospel Day.*
> (From the author's Apology for his Book)

1. The second panel represents Christian with his guide, Evangelist. Walking alone in the fields in great distress of mind, he saw a man named Evangelist coming to him, and he asked "Wherefore dost thou cry?" As Christian told him that he feared his burden of sin would sink him lower than the grave, Evangelist gave him a parchment roll and there was written therein, "Fly from the wrath to come" (Matt. 3:7). And the man said "Whither must I fly?" Then said Evangelist:

> *Do you see yonder wicket gate?*
> (Page 10, line 17)

The neighbors mock at Christian because they that fly from the wrath to come are a gazing stock to the World.

2. Led out of his way by Mr. Worldly Wiseman, Christian falls into the Slough of Despond, and Pliable leaves him. He is met again by Evangelist who reproaches him for beginning to reject the counsel of the Most High. As Christian bewails his error, Evangelist says to him:

> *Be not faithless but believing.*
> (John 20:27)

3. Christian knocks at the small wicket gate and it is opened to him by Goodwill. He had been warned by Evangelist beforehand (p. 22) "that the Lord says ,'Strive to enter in at the strait gate' (Luke 13:24), the gate to which I send thee; for

> *Strait is the Gate."*
> (Matt. 7:14)

4. Christian enters the House of the Interpreter, who holds a candle in his hand. On Interpreter's left stands his man. On being admitted and questioned he tells his errand and says that he wants to be shown excellent things that will be helpful to him on his journey. Interpreter replies:

> *I will show thee* [that which will be profitable to thee].
> (Page 28, lines 33–34)

16 The Bunyan Window,
The Bottom Tier

5. On coming to a place where stands a cross, Christian loses his burden which rolls off his back and into a sepulcher hard by (p. 38, ll. 18–19). Three Shining Ones, symbolic of the Trinity, salute him. The first says:

Thy sins be forgiven thee.
(Mark 2:5)

6. Christian goes up the Hill Difficulty. On the way he turns aside at a pleasant arbor and as he sleeps he loses the roll from his hand. When he comes to the top of the hill, he is met by Timorous and Mistrust who tell him of two lions in the way and turn back. As Christian proceeds and sees the Palace called Beautiful, he also sees the lions but the Porter tells him they are chained. While he was climbing the hill, he sang:

Better *though difficult the right way.*
(Page 42, line 7)

7. Christian goes down into the Valley of Humiliation, to the edge of which he was accompanied by the four maidens, Discretion, Piety, Charity, and Prudence from the Palace Beautiful. This panel also stands for the Valley of the Shadow of Death through which leads the way to the Celestial City. Disconsolate, Christian hears the voice of a man quoting Psalm 23:4, "though I walk through the Valley of the Shadow of Death,

I will fear no evil"
(Page 64, lines 8–9)

Large Figures of the Bottom Tier

Christian's battle with Apollyon is illustrated by their two figures, confronted in the center, left and right. "The monster was hideous to behold; he was clothed with scales like a fish . . . he had wings like a dragon and feet like a bear, and out of his belly came fire and smoke, and his mouth was as the mouth of a lion" (p. 56, ll. 23–28). Clad in the armor given him at the Palace Beautiful, and although wounded in his head, hand, and foot (Understanding, Faith, Conversation), he finally defeats the monster with the Sword of the Spirit, which is the word of God. His challenge to Apollyon is written in the glass:

Apollyon beware [what you do]
For I am on the King's Highway.
(Page 59, lines 7–8)

To the right of the two central figures is *Ignorance* of the Town of Conceit, flanked by *Obstinate* and *Pliable*, while to the left is *Worldly Wiseman* flanked by *Formalist* and *Hypocrisy*.

Panels of the Middle Tier

The panels continue from the lower left, reading horizontally as before. Panels 8 through 11 are devoted to Vanity Fair. Running through the bases of the four panels:

> *And the name of that town is Vanity; and at the*
> *town is a Fair kept, called Vanity Fair.*
> (Page 88, lines 5–6)

8. Christian and Faithful enter the town through which leads the way to the Celestial City.

9. A hubbub arises because of the Pilgrims' dress and speech, for they "naturally spoke the language of Canaan," and set little store on all the wares shown them, so that they stop their ears and on being asked what they would buy, quote from Proverbs 23:23:

> *We buy the truth.*
> (Page 90, line 19)

10. They are loaded with chains by their tormentors,
> *Some mocking, some taunting.*
> (Page 90, line 21)

11. *Faithful*, having been condemned, suffers martyrdom. "Thus came *Faithful* to his end. . . . There stood behind the multitude a chariot and a couple of horses waiting for *Faithful* who was taken up into it and straightway was carried up . . . with sound of trumpet, the nearest way to the Celestial Gate" (p. 97, ll. 20–26). Christian, freed by God, escapes and is joined by *Hopeful*.

12. Christian and Hopeful meet *Demas* who urges them to look at a silver mine in the little hill called Lucre, dangerous to travelers who fall into the mine and are maimed or killed. Hopeful was tempted but Christian held him back saying:

> *That treasure is a snare.*
> (Page 107, line 9)

13. Giant Despair brandishes his *grievous crab-tree cudgel* (p. 114, l. 21). Christian and Hopeful, led astray by Vain-Confidence, had turned aside from the way to sleep in the Giant's grounds and so they are taken by him for trespass. Through this and the following panel runs the inscription:

> *Whose Castle's Doubting and Whose Name's Despair*
> (Page 119, line 6)

14. Christian and Hopeful are imprisoned and Giant Despair, about to make an end of them, suffers one of his "fits":

For he sometimes in sunshiny weather fell into fits.
(Page 115, line 10)

15. The pilgrims escape from Doubting Castle by means of a key that Christian found he had had in his bosom all the time. As they await the Giant's return, dreading further beatings or death, Christian suddenly exclaims: What a fool am I . . .

I have a key (in my bosom) *called Promise.*
(Page 118, lines 6–7)

Large Figures of the Middle Tier

These figures represent (left center) *Christian* with *Flatterer,* "a man black of flesh but covered with a very light robe, and in his hands a net in which they were both so entangled that they knew not what to do; and with that the white robe fell off the flesh of the man's back. Then they saw where they were" (p. 133, ll. 1–3). On the other side of Christian is *Atheist,* who laughs them to scorn for their ignorance in undertaking so tedious a journey. The group typifies the temptations and trials of this part of the pilgrimage.

The panel at the center right shows *Faithful,* who had accompanied Christian as far as Vanity Fair. With him are *Talkative,* who "deceiveth his own soul," and *Wanton,* of "baleful seductiveness," . . . both of whom were powerless against Faithful.

The left-hand panel shows *Interpreter,* dressed as a minister of the Gospel with small opposing figures of *Money-Love* and his friend *By-Ends.*

The right-hand panel shows *Evangelist* opposed by small figures of *Hold-the-World* and *Save-All.* Having come up with Christian and Faithful and heard all that had happened to them on the way, he exhorted them to hold out, saying:

The Crown is before you.
(Page 86, line 31)

Panels of the Top Tier

Beginning at the lower left, the panels continue.

16. Christian and Hopeful reach the Delectable Mountains, or attain Peace of Soul. They are received by the Shepherds of this Emmanuel's Land: Knowledge, Experience, Watchful, and Sincere, about whom are the sheep, His Redeemed. The pilgrims look through the Perspective Glass at the Mount called Clear and seeing the Celestial City afar off, are told:

Solace yourselves [with the good of these Delectable Mountains].
(Page 120, lines 15–16)

17. Christian and Hopeful cross the River of Death. Christian at first began to sink, crying: "I sink in Deep Waters, the Billows go over my head,

all his Waves go over me" (p. 157, ll. 10–11). As they emerge, having left their mortal garments behind them in the river, they are pursued by two small demons, who then fly away. The inscription is for both panels 18 and 19.

We pass out of this world into Glory

18. Christian and Hopeful are received by two Shining Ones, who lead them up to the Celestial City of which they say the beauty and glory are inexpressible.

19. Enoch, Moses, and Elijah look down from above the Gate of Heaven (p. 161). To them were given the pilgrims' certificates to be carried to the King, who commanded that the gate be opened

> *That the Righteous Nation* [that keepeth truth]
> *may enter in.*
>
> (Isa. 26:2)

Large Figures of the Top Tier

Above these panels are four figures: *Discretion* "A grave and beautiful damsel," *Piety, Charity,* and *Prudence,* all dwellers in the Palace Beautiful, whose help and counsel were of such avail to Christian. They are surrounded by "servants and engines," souvenirs of the maids' discourse with Christian in the Palace Beautiful: *Moses* and his rod, *Jael's* hammer and nail, *Gideon's* pitchers and lamps, *Shamgar's* ox-goad, *Samson* and the jawbone of the ass, *David* and his sling, *Samuel* with a jar of ointment and *Isaiah* with tongues and coals of fire.

Above these are Christian (left center) and Hopeful (right center) with harps and "raiment that shone like gold," with small figures of "Shining Ones" on either side of them. Far right and left are the "King's Trumpeters," who saluted Christian and his fellow "with ten thousand welcomes from the world and this they did with Shouting and Trumpets." In the midst of these there are figures on either side of the Shining Ones, with crowns in token of honor, which they tender toward Christian and Hopeful (p. 162). Running through the four divisions are the words said to them:

> *Enter ye into the joy of Our Lord.*
> (Matt. 25:23)

In the upper central tracery piece is God the Son, the Redeemer, Emmanuel with the Sheep, His Redeemed; in the small piece immediately below is the Candle of Interpreter. Angels, Trumpeters, and Ringing Bells fill the other tracery pieces and complete the composition with the words:

> *Holy, Holy, Holy is the Lord.*
> (Page 162, line 19)

THE NAVE: SOUTH SIDE

26. *Sixth Bay.* Philosophy

In the rose at the top Zeus represents the wisdom to which the philosophers looked. Below are large figures with, above each, a symbol associated with him. From left to right: Pythagoras (Lyre), Demosthenes (Cosmic World), Plato (head of Athena, goddess of Wisdom), Aristotle (Head of Alexander, his most famous pupil), Francis Bacon (a pair of scales). Below are later philosophers. In the same order they are Spinoza, Hume, Berkeley, Descartes, Kant.

27. *Fifth Bay.* Theology

In the rose at the top: Jesus teaches Nicodemus, a Pharisee and a ruler of the Jews.

> Rabbi, we know that thou art a teacher come from
> God for no man can do these miracles.
>
> (John 3:2)

The symbols in the small lights on either side are, to the left, the lamp of Christian knowledge, set between the pillars of wisdom, with the monogram of Christ, XP, above; to the right, the Torah revitalized and spread by St. Paul's *spiritus gladius* (the Sword of the Spirit). Five figures in the lancets represent the great teachers of Theology. From left to right:

st. paul. Above him the symbol of the three fountains of wisdom.

st. athanasius. The symbol is an open book.

st. thomas aquinas, author of the *Summa Theologica* with the symbol of a sheaf of wheat and a wine chalice.

john calvin, holding his book on the Institutes of Christian Religion, 1536. Above him, the symbol of a heart proffered by an outstretched hand.

jonathan edwards, for a few months in 1758 President of the College of New Jersey, symbolized by the seal of the University, as well as by the seal of the Yale Divinity School whence he had graduated in 1720.

In the panels below the figures are symbolized the five great affirmations of the New Testament which form the pillars of Reform Theology:

1. "Justification by faith": a serpent typifying sin, forgiven by reconciliation with God.

2. The Priesthood of all Believers: shown by the globe of the world and the scallop shell, symbolic of baptism.

3. The Primary Authority of the Bible, shown here as open, diffusing knowledge as a cross-topped lamp diffuses light.

4. The "Right of Private Judgment" is shown by a heart and a balance or scales that weighs Scripture against the heart.

5. The Sacredness of every vocation. The symbol of marriage as a vocation requiring greater self-sacrifice than most is shown by the intertwined lamps.

28. *Fourth Bay.* Chivalry

The discipline is symbolized by five figures. From left to right they are:

ROLAND. On the shield above, an ivory horn recalls the summons he blew at Roncevaux to call back aid from Charlemagne's army, for which he and his companions formed the rear guard. The scene below suggests the battle.

RICHARD THE LION-HEARTED, crusader. His arms of the three leopards (*passant guardant*) are shown on the shield above. In the scene below he turns away so as not to see the Holy City to which he could not attain.

GODFREY DE BOUILLON, leader of the first Crusade and first Christian King of Jerusalem. At his feet lies the crown he refused to wear in the city where Christ had been crowned with thorns. This crown he holds before him. Above are his arms, and below is the Church of the Holy Sepulcher.

BERTRAND DE BORNE, troubador, to whom is attributed the "Roman de la Rose," which is symbolized on the shield above his head. In the panel below he appears as a minstrel with a harp.

BERTRAND DU GUESCLIN, Constable of France and hero of the fourteenth century. The device of the double eagle on his shield identified him to the chivalry of his time. The panel shows him as a tomb figure. In the rose at the top of the window a mounted knight recalls the type of seal common at that time.

29. *Third Bay.* Poetry

The brilliant glass of this window is devoted to the depiction of poets from ancient to modern times.

In the rose at the top is KING DAVID, as a psalmist, playing his harp and singing. The two trefoils below, to left and right, show MARTIN LUTHER translating the Bible and GEORGE HERBERT, seventeenth century poet and a pupil of Donne. ("Who plainly say my God, my King.")

In the left lancet stands VERGIL pointing to the Holy Child of the Fourth Eclogue, whose advent shall renew the world. He stands on Parnassus and holds the lilies of Aeneid IV to recall that line "Give me handfuls of lilies," which DANTE, who appears in the second lancet, heard spoken by the Church Triumphant at the opening of Paradise. Dante is shown as an aged exile for whom Vergil's Holy Child was the Prophesied Christ. Below Dante is CHAUCER, who introduced Dante to England, shown with Canterbury cathedral. SHAKESPEARE is at the top of the central lancet, and below him JOHN DONNE, as Dean of St. Paul's, holding a chalice and a book with a heart. JOHN

MILTON, old and blind, in the fourth lancet, is symbolically carrying a Bible, which he valued above all other books. WILLIAM BLAKE, below him, is drawing, and shown with his "Tyger" and the arrows of desire and the bow of burning gold of his "Preface to Milton." At the extreme right is EMILY DICKINSON, her great concerns, nature and death, symbolized by the flaming sun ("I reckon when I count all") and the gravestone on which she sits. The purple flower she holds recalls her poem "Of death I try to think like this." Below her, T. S. ELIOT climbs a turning stair as in "Ash Wednesday III," lighting his way with a eucharistic candle.

30. *Second Bay.* Law

This discipline is symbolized by five principal figures, above each of whom is an appropriate device and in the panel below a typical scene. They are, from left to right:

AUGUSTUS, in military dress. On his cuirass may be seen the chariot of the sun, with a representation of the sky god above. His symbol is a Roman standard with the letters S.P.Q.R. Below he is shown as Pontifex Maximus, sacrificing, with the words *Caesar Augustus.*

JUSTINIAN in imperial robes. Above him the monogram of Christ, XP. Below is a scene inscribed *Justinian instructs . . . to codify the Law.*

The central figure is ST. LOUIS (IX), King of France. The arms of France (ancient: a blue field sown with fleur de lys) appear above his head. Below he is seen *Dispensing Justice at Vincennes.* To his left is GROTIUS. Above him is repeated twice the device of three trumpets with an inescutcheon charged with a six-pointed star. Below he is shown with the inscription *Hugo Grotius codifies International Law.*

Next is JAMES MADISON with the arms of Princeton University above him (they are an intentional anachronism since they were not adopted until 1897). Below he is shown with the inscription *Madison drafts the Constitution.*

31. *First Bay.* Science

Three figures dominate the central lancets: HIPPOCRATES, the Father of Medicine; ARISTOTLE, "the master of those who know," whose courage in adventuring far in search of truth marks the true scientific spirit and is symbolized by a brilliant true red, as distinct from the cool blue (wisdom) of the other figures; ROGER BACON, who typifies the mediaeval scientific spirit that unites devout religious feeling with earnest insistence upon reason and experiment in the pursuit of truth.

Starting at the upper left, continuing down and across the base and terminating in the upper right lancet head, eleven panels form a series dedicated to other great pioneers of science. These are treated as symbolic subjects typifying one significant achievement of each figure:

1. ARISTARCHUS of Samos, the great pioneer astronomer, holds a pair of dividers, symbolizing his method of measuring heavenly bodies.

2. EUCLID, father of Geometry, holds a triangle, to recall his most famous theorem.

3. ARCHIMEDES, the great natural scientist, is represented conducting his famous experiment in hydrostatics, the detection of silver alloy in the crown of King Hieron.

4. GALEN the "wonderworker," who was the greatest student of anatomy after Hippocrates, is shown dissecting.

5. PTOLEMY, who first used trigonometry for astrological calculation, is shown recording his discoveries on a monument which he is said to have erected near Alexandria.

6. GALILEO, the picturesque Renaissance scientist, holds a telescope and a pendulum symbolizing two of his many fields of activity.

7. PASCAL, type of all theologian-scientists, holds a barometer, significant of his study of atmospheric pressure.

8. NEWTON is represented near his celebrated apple tree, recalling his first realization of the laws governing falling bodies.

9. HARVEY, who discovered the nature of the circulation of the blood, is shown studying a symbolic diagram of the heart and arteries.

10. PASTEUR holds two flasks representing the experiment by which he proved the organic source of fermentation and infection.

11. JOSEPH HENRY, one of America's leading scientists and students of electricity, also reorganized our lighthouse system making it one of the finest in the world. The symbolic figure of a lighthouse appears beside him in the panel. He was Professor of Natural Philosophy at Princeton, 1832–1842.

At the top of each of the four side lancets appear the symbols of the four natural elements: Earth (the square) and Water (the circle), on the left; Fire (the triangle) and Air (the jewel and crescent), on the right. These ancient symbols are older than Christianity, as is also the Egyptian *Crux Ansata* in the center, symbol of the life-giving principle, the union of flesh and spirit, and of immortality.

An allegorical figure of *Scientia*, suggesting Athena, Goddess of Wisdom and Humanity, appears in the central tracery member. Surrounding this are six small pieces in which are the twelve signs of the zodiac. In the two trefoils appear symbols related to Athens: the figure of Nike, Goddess of Victory, and the cadeuceus, symbol of insight into the mystery of life and death, since it was carried by Hermes, who conducted the spirits of the departed to the other world. The background of the entire window is delicately traced in a pattern of olive branches, suggesting the wreath of victory.

32. *Sixth Bay.* The Sermon on the Mount, with the Beatitudes

Christ is shown in the upper part of the central lancet. The inscription: *He opened his mouth and taught them* (Matt. 5:2).

To his left, in the upper register: *Blessed are the meek* (Matt. 5:5).

To the right: *Blessed are the merciful* (Matt. 5:7).

Across the window in the lower register are:

Blessed are the pure in heart (Matt. 5:8).

Blessed are they that mourn (Matt. 5:4).

Blessed are the poor in spirit (Matt. 5:3).

33. *Fifth Bay.* The Sermon on the Mount, with five episodes portrayed

Christ is shown in the top central lancet which is inscribed: *He went up into a moun(tain)* (Matt. 5:1).

To the left: *Knock and it shall be opened* (Matt. 7:7).

To the right: *First be thou reconciled* (Matt. 5:24).

In the lower register of the lancets are:

Do not give alms before men (Matt. 6:1).

Built his house on a rock (Matt. 7:24).

Good Tree bringeth forth good fruit (Matt. 7:17).

34. *Fourth Bay.* The Parable of the Wedding Feast

In the central panel, at the top, is written: *The Marriage Feast* (Matt. 22:2), that was given by the King for his Son.

To the left is the guest who: *Refuses to come* (Matt. 22:3). On the right, the King commands his servants: *Go ye into the highways* (Matt. 22:9) and the lower section, on the right, illustrates his order: *As many as ye shall find bid to the wedding* (Matt. 22:9). In the center is a guest who came, *And had not on a wedding garment* (Matt. 22:11). Then the King said to his servants (lower left) "Bind him *and cast him into outer darkness*" (Matt. 22:13), "and there shall be weeping and gnashing of teeth, For many are called but few are chosen" (Matt. 22:13–14).

35. *Third Bay.* The Parable of the Ten Talents

The key to the parable is in the top center with the inscription: *The Lord of those servants cometh* (Matt. 25:19). Below, at the foot of the window, he is shown starting on his journey to a far country, having called his servants to him, *and delivered unto them his goods* (Matt. 25:14). On the lower right is the servant who was entrusted with five talents (Matt. 25:16), *The five talents man trades.* On the lower left is the man who received one talent *and hid his Lord's money* (Matt. 25:18). In the upper left, when the master had returned, the first servant returns the original five talents *and brought other five talents* (Matt. 25:20). The figure on the upper right represents the unprofitable servant who merely hid the money, and returned it saying: *Here thou hast which is thine* (Matt. 25:25), whereupon his master ordered that he be cast out and the talent he returned given to the man who had ten talents. "For unto every one that hath shall be given . . . but from him that hath not shall be taken away even that which he hath" (Matt. 25:29).

36. *Second Bay.* The Parable of the Wise and the Foolish Virgins

This, and the preceding parables, are intended to teach the expectation of the Second Coming of the Lord, which is portrayed in the Great West Window (37).

The key is given in the upper part of the central lancet: *The Bridegroom cometh* (Matt. 25:6) "go ye out to meet him." In the center of the lower register all the ten virgins are sleeping. At the upper left, *Five were wise* (Matt. 25:2); and at the right, *Five were foolish* (Matt. 25:2). At the lower left are shown the foolish ones who sought too late to replenish their lamps, for which they had not provided oil. While *they went to buy* (Matt. 25:10) the bridegroom came and the door was shut. On the right they cry: *Lord open to us* (Matt. 25:11), but he answered, "Verily I say unto you, I know you not. Watch therefore, for ye know neither the day nor the hour when the Son of man cometh" (Matt. 25:12–13).

THE GALLERY

37. *The Great West Window.* The Second Coming of Christ

The West Window (37)
Color plate, page 22

The inscription that gives the motif for this window is carved on the central section of the rail of the higher gallery *I am come that they might have life and that they might have it more abundantly* (John 10:10). To left and right of the central section are carved, respectively: *In thy light we shall see light* (Ps. 36:9), and *I am the way, the truth and the life* (John 14:6). Christ, the central figure, is seated in a mandorla decorated with the signs of the Zodiac to show that he comprehends all time. He is clothed in a garment of light. The Zodiac, reading from the lower left clockwise, shows *Cancer, Leo, Virgo, Libra, Capricor* (nus), *Aquari* (us), *P* (is)*ce* (s), and *T* (au)*rus*, each with its appropriate symbol. Christ's feet rest upon the Lion, under which is a Lamb. On the inner border of the mandorla is written *I will give him that is athirst the waters of life* (Rev. 21:6). Below, angels with great trumpets summon the elect. In the lower register the three central panels show the Nativity of Jesus—the first coming; in the center, the Virgin and Child with the Star of Bethlehem above. To left and right are the Three Wise Men and the Shepherds.

98

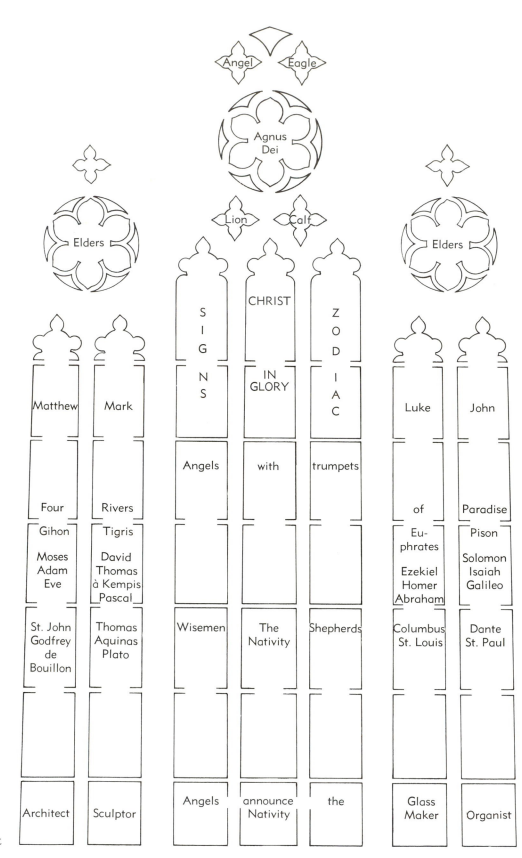

Angel   Eagle

Agnus
Dei

Lion   Calf

Elders

Elders

S I G N S	CHRIST	Z O D I A C		Luke	John
	IN GLORY				
Angels	with	trumpets		of	Paradise
Four	Rivers			Eu- phrates	Pison
Gihon	Tigris				
Moses Adam Eve	David Thomas à Kempis Pascal			Ezekiel Homer Abraham	Solomon Isaiah Galileo
Wisemen	The Nativity	Shepherds		Columbus St. Louis	Dante St. Paul
St. John Godfrey de Bouillon	Thomas Aquinas Plato				
Angels	announce Nativity	the		Glass Maker	Organist
Architect	Sculptor				

Matthew   Mark

**The Great West Window:
The Second Coming of Christ**

In the tops of the lancets flanking the three central ones are the Evangelists: Matthew, with the words *Thou art Christ* inscribed on the book he holds; Mark, who carries a scroll on which is written *There is one God— none other*. Luke, also with a scroll inscribed *Call his name Jesus*, and John on whose book are the words *Lord God*. Under each Evangelist is one of the Rivers of Paradise: *Gihon, Tigris, Euphr(ates)* and *Pison*.

In the lower register are gathered many of the figures shown elsewhere in the windows, mystically present at the Second Coming; soldiers, philosophers, doctors, and poets. Each is identified by an inscription. In the first lancet to the left are *Moses, Adam, Eve, St. John* (identified by the inscription *Ecce Agnus Dei*), and *Godfrey de Bouillon*, first Christian King of Jerusalem. In the second lancet are *David*, Thomas à Kempis (identified by the words *Imitatio Christi), Pascal, Thomas Aquin*(as) holding his Summa Theologica, and *Plato*. The first lancet to the right of the three central ones shows *Ezekiel*, Homer (identified by the *Iliad* he holds), *Abraham, Columbus, St. Louis*. In the lancet beside it are *Solomon, Isaiah, Galileo, Dante* holding his Divine Comedy, and *Paul*.

Below the figures and all across the window is written: *Blessings— Honor: Glory—Power: Be unto Him: That Sitteth: upon the Throne: unto the Lamb: for Ever and Ever* (Rev. 5:13).

Seven small panels under the inscription represent, at the left, the architect, the sculptor, angels announcing the Nativity to the Shepherds (three panels), the glass painter, and the organist. The first two and last two are, of course, the artists involved in the building of the chapel.

Returning to the tracery at the top of the window, in the top center is the Lamb of God surrounded by the Seven Lamps of Wisdom; small openings to either side contain cherubim, and above and below are four openings with the symbols of the Evangelists. The two smaller panels contain the four and twenty elders casting down their crowns before the throne (Rev. 4:12–13). Around each panel is inscribed:

> *Thou art worthy, O Lord, to receive Glory*
> *Thou art worthy, O Lord, to receive Honor*

THE NARTHEX

38. Medicine

Medicine is represented by the Persian-born Mohammedan physician al-Rāzi, who holds a scroll that indicates his general treatise on medicine. The inscription may be translated, "The Book of Everything [on Medicine]," and underneath, "In the name of Allah, the Merciful, the Compassionate." This work influenced medical science in the Middle Ages and was translated, along with other important works of his, into Latin. The physician's name is inscribed in the glass at the lower right.

The Arts
(windows 38–40)
Plate 17

17 Al-Razi, The Arab Physician, Narthex   18 St. John of Damascus, Narthex

39. Music   Plate 18

Music is represented by the figure of St. John of Damascus, theologian
and writer, who organized liturgical song in the Eastern Church.

Διὰ πάντος εὐλογοῦντες
ὁ ἅγιος Ἰωάννης Δαμασκινός

40. Painting

Painting is represented by Fra Angelico, Dominican friar, who painted
frescoes as subjects for contemplation in the cells at the convent of San
Marco in Florence.

Beato Angelico da Fiesole

41. The Holy Family   *The Narthex Stairway*
                                                                             (window 41)

Lighting the stairs that lead from the north and south ends of the
narthex to the gallery are two windows illustrating the Book of Job. Beginning with the window of the north stair, the familiar story is read upward
in each lancet and from the left.

42. *North window*   *The Gallery Stairways*
                                                                             (windows 42-43)
The first, smaller panel introduces the prosperous Job—"greatest of all   *The Book of Job*
men of the east" (1:3). Satan approaches from one side. The larger medal-   Plates 19 and 20
lion just above represents his seven sons, feasting (1:4). Above this, the
Sabeans steal his oxen (1:15).

In the dominant panel, Satan comes before the Lord, who carries the
globe surmounted by the Cross as a symbol of domination over the world;
"Hast thou considered my servant Job? . . . All that he hath is in thy power."
(1:6-12). At the top, Job offers burnt sacrifice (1:5). On the altar is represented the Phoenix, rising anew from the flames of its nest.

In the base of the second panel, fire destroys the sheep. Evil spirits with
firebrands appear on either side. Next above, the great wind destroys Job's
sons (1:8) and above are shown the Chaldeans carrying off his camels (1:17).

In the large panel Job still praises God (1:20–21); Satan watches. At the
top, Job is shorn of everything and is still plagued by evil spirits.

In the quatrefoil above, Job stands bearing the text, *The Lord gave,
and the Lord hath taken away; blessed be the name of the Lord* (1:21).

43. *South window*

At the foot of the left panel, Job, covered with boils, sits in the ashes
while his wife counsels him to curse God and die (2:8–9). Satan points upward as though to say that the worst is yet to come. In the larger panel above,

19 The Book of Job,
North Stair Window

20 The Book of Job,
South Stair Window

Job's three friends Eliphas, Bildad, and Zophar come to comfort and mourn with him, while Elihu stands by (2:11–13). Job turns his head away. The smaller panel next above shows Job besieged with woe from all sides; he justifies his complaint, "the arrows of the Almighty are within me" (6:4).

The top panel shows God, answering Job out of the whirlwind. "Who is this that darkeneth counsel by words without knowledge?"—"Shall he that contendeth with the Almighty instruct Him?" (Chapters 38–40).

Leviathan opens the second lancet. He is flanked by other wild creatures, mighty and awesome works of God. This theme is enlarged upon above and in the companion panel with the wild goat, the peacock, ostrich, unicorn and hind, as well as with the mountains and the sea (top of first panel). "Whatsoever is under the whole heaven is mine" (41:11).

Above, God has forgiven the humbled and repentant Job. He is surrounded by his sons and daughters, and the harvest lies at his feet.

In the top large panel the wrathful God commands the three friends to take Job seven bullocks and seven rams for a burnt offering (42:7–8). In the little medallion below, Job prays for his friends over the burnt offering they have made (42:10). Above the large panel, Job, blessed by the Lord, sits in prosperity and contentment.

In the quatrefoil, Job, surrounded by the sun, moon, and stars holds a scroll inscribed: *Yet will I trust in Him* (13:15).

Commentary.

I am indebted to Mr. Orin E. Skinner, President of Charles J. Connick Associates, for the description of these windows, prepared from notes, correspondence, and diagrams. Some extracts from the correspondence of Professor Friend with the artist are illustrative of the close connection he always maintained with the work. "I remember that I was inspired for some of the iconography by the little metal cuts in Pigouchet's printed Book of Hours of the late xv century. . . . In this book Pigouchet plays the Book of Job against the Dance of Death as an argument against suicide. . . . Let's stay away from Blake. His nature mysticism is far from the essential spirit of the Hebrew author." Commenting on the sketches and referring to Job completely dejected, he wrote: "His hoary head is *turned away* from his friends. I think this is an excellent idea and should be preserved. In the central scene of the left light Job should justify his complaint by raising his arms in gesticulation *against* God as it were. Only this will justify God's terrible and immediate appearance above in the whirlwind. I would get rid of a special Job and Elihu panel. Elihu was about as bad as the other friends, and the whole Elihu episode is an interpolation into the original book anyhow."

With reference to the Job windows in the whole cycle of the windows, he wrote: "This is really the most important book of the Old Testament and the last of the literary cycles in the Chapel. I am very anxious that the students be able to make it out."

SOUTH VESTIBULE

44. The Tree in the Storm

The Crypt Stairway (window 44)

At the head of the stair leading up from the crypt is a window in memory of Adlai E. Stevenson, Class of 1922. It represents a tree attacked by fire and storm. The crushing and consuming threat is met by the thrust and surge of life. It is intended to typify the awareness and courage with which Stevenson faced life, in the faith that highest principles can ultimately prevail.

45. Symbolic Flowers and Plants

The Southeast Porch (window 45)

In the tympanum of the southeast porch are four small quatrefoils of faceted glass, in which are represented certain flowers and plants traditionally used in Christian symbolism. In the quatrefoil at the top (see frontispiece) ivy, which stands for death, immortality, and fidelity, bisects the quatrefoil, with the strawberry (perfect righteousness) at the left and the rose (triumphant love and martyrdom) at the right. Reading the quatrefoils clockwise, one finds in the next the olive branch at the center (peace and healing), with the thistle (sorrow, sin, and Christ's Passion) at the left and the pomegranate (Resurrection) at the right. The next quatrefoil contains a palm branch (the victory of martyrs) at the center, with grapes (the blood of Christ, the True Vine) at the left and the lily (purity and the Annunciation) at the right. The next quatrefoil contains the laurel branch (triumph and chastity) at the center, with the almond (divine approval) at the left and the violet (humility) at the right.

MEMORIAL GIFTS

Compiled by Frederic E. Fox,
Recording Secretary of the University

MEMORIAL GIFTS

MEMORIAL gifts are grouped, as far as is practicable, under categories (Doorways, Windows, Pews, Inscriptions, Lanterns, Paneling, Organs, Furnishings) with the names of the persons commemorated, and the donors. The general order is from west to east, except that the windows follow the numbering as given on the plan. Memorials outside the chapel are listed last.

The *Auditory System* is the gift of Archibald A. Gulick, Thomas C. Dunham, Murray G. Day, Walter L. Johnson, Andrew Mills, Jr., Harry C. Robb, and Frederick Sturges, Jr., all of the Class of 1897. *Memorial Flower Funds* have been established in memory of Harold Sydney Edwards, Class of 1906, by Harold S. Edwards, Jr., Class of 1933, and C. William Edwards, Class of 1936; and in memory of Adlai E. Stevenson, Class of 1922, by his sister, Mrs. Ernest I. Ives.

DOORWAYS

IN MEMORY OF	DONOR/ARTIST	LOCATION
Pyne, Robert Stockton and Pyne Jr. 1908, M. Taylor The inscription reads: *This portal is given by Mrs. M. Taylor Pyne/ in memory of her two sons/ Robert Stockton Pyne and M. Taylor Pyne Jr.*	DONOR: Pyne, Mrs. M. Taylor ARTIST: John Angel	*Portal of West Facade*
Campbell 1894, James Shaw	DONOR: Campbell, Mrs. William O.	*North Aisle Door*
Frame 1897, John Musser	DONOR: Frame, Mrs. Florence Rick ARTIST: John Angel	*Northwest Door Tympanum*
Poe 1854, Mr. and Mrs. John P.	DONOR: Poe 1897, Neilson	*Southeast Door*
Betts, Mr. and Mrs. George W.	DONOR: Betts Jr. 1892, George W.	*North Central Door*
Horton, Loton	DONORS: Horton 1903, Daniel S. Horton 1906, Chauncey T. Horton 1910, Ralph B. Horton 1915, Jerome L. ARTIST: Robert Baker	*Southwest Door Tympanum*

MEMORIAL WINDOWS

The windows are listed according to their numbers on the plan and in the text. The memorial inscriptions, printed here in italics, are either incorporated in the glass or placed nearby on the wall of the chapel.

Window 1	On a stone to the left of the door leading down from the gallery: *The Clerestory window above is given in reverent/ gratitude for the lives of/ Catherine Plant Judson Holden/ Katherine Judson Holden Sutton/ Frederick Judson Holden Sutton/ Class of 1898*	DONOR: Sutton 1898, F.J.H. ARTIST: Henry Lee Willet
Window 2	On a stone of the aisle wall below: *The Clerestory window above is given/ to the Glory of God/ and in loving memory of my father/ Van Dyke B. Gulick/ and my mother/ Julia Downing Gulick/ Archibald A. Gulick '97*	DONOR: Gulick 1897, Archibald A. ARTIST: Henry Lee Willet
Window 3	On a stone in the aisle wall below: *The Clerestory window above/ is given in memory of/ Henry M. Alexander/ a trustee of the University/ by his son Maitland Alexander/ Class of 1889*	DONOR: Alexander 1889, Maitland ARTIST: Oliver Smith
Window 4	In the glass at the foot of the window: *In memory of Harvey Lawrence Cory, Class of 1917*	DONOR: Cory, Mr. and Mrs. Harvey
Window 5	In the glass at the foot of the window: *In loving memory of William Mortimer Matthews, Class/ of 1878* On the aisle wall below the window: *The Clerestory window above/ is in memory of/ Mortimer Matthews/ June 22, 1858 – September 1, 1927*	DONOR: Matthews 1887, Paul ARTIST: Oliver Smith
Window 6	In the glass at the foot of the window: *MDCCCLIX to the Glory of God in loving memory/ of Cyrus Hall McCormick MCMXXXVI*	DONOR: McCormick, Mrs. Cyrus Hall ARTIST: Charles J. Connick
Window 7	In the glass at the foot of the window: *In memory of John Baxter Black, Class of 1971*	DONORS: Black, Mr. and Mrs. Edward ARTIST: Wilbur Herbert Burnham

In the glass at the foot of the window: *In memory of Clarence Boyd Maxwell Garrigues, Class of 1920*	DONOR: Garrigues Jr. 1919, William A. ARTIST: Wilbur Herbert Burnham	*Window 8*
In the glass at the foot of the window: *In memory of James Hay Reed LHD 1902*	DONOR: Reed 1900, David A. ARTIST: Wilbur Herbert Burnham	*Window 9*
In the glass at the foot of the window: *In memory of Charles Kellogg Backus, Class of 1861*	DONOR: Backus, Standish ARTIST: Wilbur Herbert Burnham	*Window 10*
In memory of Cornelius C. Cuyler, Class of 1879	DONOR: Cuyler, Eleanor De Graff ARTIST: G. Gerard Recke	*Windows 11, 12*
In memory of Frederick Alexander Marquand, Class of 1876	ARTIST: Oliver Smith	*Window 13*
In the glass at the foot of the window: *Horatio Whitridge Garrett, Class of 1895*	DONORS: Garrett 1897, Robert; Garrett 1895, John W. ARTISTS: Joseph G. Reynolds Jr., William M. Francis, J. Henry Rohnstock	*Window 14*
In the glass at the foot of the window: *In memory of John Thomas Duffield, Class of 1841/ Born February 19, 1823 Died April 10, 1901*	DONOR: Duffield 1892, Edward D. ARTISTS: Joseph G. Reynolds Jr., William M. Francis, J. Henry Rohnstock	*Window 15*
In memory of Margaret G. and David M. Dillon	DONOR: Dillon 1907, Herbert Lowell ARTIST: H. J. Butler	*Window 16*
In memory of William Earle Dodge, Jr., Class of 1879	DONOR: Mrs. William E. Dodge ARTIST: H. W. Goodhue	*Window 17*
In memory of Herbert E. Rankin, Class of 1909	DONOR: Rankin, Catherine ARTIST: H. W. Goodhue	*Window 18*
In memory of Elizabeth Milbank Anderson	DONOR: Milbank Memorial Fund ARTIST: H. W. Goodhue	*Windows 19, 20*
For the inscription in the stone below the window, see page 9.	DONOR: Milbank Memorial Fund ARTIST: Charles J. Connick	*Window 21*
These windows form a part of the Milbank Memorial	ARTIST: Charles J. Connick	*Windows 22, 23, 24, 25*
In the stone of the aisle wall below the window is the inscription: *The clerestory window above/ is given in honor of/ President John Grier Hibben/ by the Board of Trustees*	DONORS: Trustees of Princeton University ARTIST: Frank Ellsworth Weeder	*Window 26*

Window 27	In the stone of the aisle wall below the window: *The clerestory window above/ is given in memory of/ Charles R. Erdman, 1886/ By his family*	DONOR: Erdman 1915, C. Pardee ARTIST: Henry Lee Willet
Window 28	On the stone of the aisle wall below the window: *The clerestory window above and the bay/ are in memory of/ Lieutenant James Jackson Porter/ Class of 1911/ Killed in action October 5, 1918*	DONOR: Porter, William E. ARTIST: Frank Ellsworth Weeder
Window 29	On the stone of the aisle wall in the bay below the window: *For the Glory of God/ The clerestory window of the poets/ is given in memory of/ Hugh Leander Adams/ and/ Mary Trumbull Adams/ by their son, Hugh Trumbull Adams, 1935*	DONOR: Adams 1935, Hugh Trumbull ARTISTS: Irene and Rowan Le Compte
Window 30	The inscription in the glass reads: *In memory of John O. H. Pitney, Class of 1881*	DONORS: Pitney, Hardin and Skinner ARTIST: Frank Ellsworth Weeder
Window 31	Inscribed on the stone to the right of the door leading down from the gallery: *In memory of George Allaire Howe, Class of 1878*	DONOR: Howe, Mrs. George A. ARTIST: Charles J. Connick
Window 32	At the foot of the window, in the glass: *In memory of Henry Nelson Pierce, Class of 1925*	DONORS: Pierce, Mr. and Mrs. Edward ARTIST: Wilbur Herbert Burnham
Window 33	In the glass at the foot of the window: *John Ballantine Pitney, 1914/ Henry Cooper Pitney, 1848/ Mahlon Pitney, 1879*	DONOR: Pitney 1881, John O. H. ARTIST: Wilbur Herbert Burnham
Window 34	In the glass at the foot of the window: *In honor of Ralph Adams Cram, Architect*	DONOR: Armour 1877, George Allison ARTIST: Wilbur Herbert Burnham
Window 35	In the glass at the foot of the window: *In memory of Nathaniel Burt, 1839/ Horace Brooke Burt, 1873/ Alfred Farmer Burt, 1882*	DONORS: The Misses Burt ARTIST: Wilbur Herbert Burnham

In the glass at the foot of the window:
*In memory of William Smith Miles,
Class of 1899*

DONOR: Miles, Mrs. William Smith
ARTIST: Wilbur Herbert Burnham

Window 36

In the glass at the foot of the window:
*In memory of Moses Taylor Pyne,
Class of 1877*

DONOR: Pyne Jr. 1908, Moses Taylor
ARTIST: Nicola d'Ascenzo

Window 37

On the stone to the right of 38:
*In memoriam/ Paul H. Ludington,
1894,/ Univ. of Penn. M.D. 1897/
1872-1932*

DONOR: McKeen, Mrs. Mary Ludington
ARTIST: Charles J. Connick

Windows 38, 39

*In memory of Sydney Richmond
Taber 1883*

DONOR: Taber, Mrs. Sydney R.
ARTIST: Charles J. Connick

Window 40

On the stone of the reveal alongside
the window:
*Given in Memory of/ Arthur J.
Horton/ by his son, Class of 1942*

DONOR: Horton Jr. 1942, Arthur J.
ARTIST: Ellen Simon

Window 41

In the glass at the foot of the window:
David Mixsell, Class of 1947
Near the inscription is the insignia of
his Division, the 30th. The O and H
stand for "Old Hickory" and the
triple X for the number of the
Division. In the corner of the panel
at the right is depicted the ribbon of
his Purple Heart Award.

DONOR: Mixsell 1915, Donald G.
ARTIST: Charles J. Connick

Window 42

In the glass:
David Mixsell, Class of 1871

DONOR: Mixsell 1915, Donald G.
ARTIST: Charles J. Connick

Window 43

The decorative glass in the tracery
above the door is a memorial to Julia
Biddle Tabor

DONOR: Poe, Mrs. John P.
ARTIST: Henry Lee Willet

Window 44

Inscribed on the stone beside the
window:
*Adlai E. Stevenson '22/ . . . Like a
tree planted by/ the rivers of Water/
Psalm I*

DONORS: Mrs. Ernest I. (Elizabeth S.)
Ives, and classmates and friends
ARTIST: Ellen Simon

Window 45

PEWS

The pews in the nave are numbered from front to back, beginning in the central aisle: odd numbers, 1–99, on the south; and even numbers, 2–100, on the north. The numbering then resumes at the front and continues to the rear, reading from the side aisles, 101–201 and 102–202. The pews that are curtailed by the columns do not have numbers cut on them but are included in the count. In the Braman Transept they are lettered A–L; and in the Marquand Transept, N–X. The gallery pews are numbered G-1 to G-20. The dedications are cut on the backs of the pews.

LOCATION		IN MEMORY OF	DONOR
Nave			
	1	Goodrich, Casper F.	Goodrich, Mrs. Casper F.
	2	Bayard 1779, Andrew Bayard, John Bubenheim	Bayard 1885, James Wilson
	3	Palmer, Susan Flanders	Palmer 1903, Edgar
	4	Henry 1813, John S.	Henry, Mrs. Bayard
	5	Wintringer, Mary F.	Wintringer 1894, George C.
	6	Henry, T. Charlton	Henry, T. Charlton
	7	Leonard, Elizabeth D. D.	Leonard 1896, Thomas D.
	8	Henry 1876, Bayard	Henry, Mrs. Bayard
	9	Murray 1866, Logan C.	Murray, A. Gordon
	10	Henry 1904, Howard Houston	Henry 1876, Bayard
	11	McKelvy, David	McKelvy, Robert
	12	Henry 1870, Alexander	Henry, Bayard
	13	Mackenzie, Jean	Fish, Raymond T.
	14	Paxton, William Miller	Roberts 1914, William Paxton
	15	World War I Dead	Anonymous
	16	Bullock III 1916, Benjamin	Roberts Jr. 1916, Frank C.
	17		Class of 1917
	18	Paxton 1891, Harmar Denny	Roberts 1921, Harmar D.
	19	Imbrie 1900, Harold	LeBoutillier 1900, Philip
	20	Roberts, William	Roberts 1883, Frank C.
	21	Hope, Isabella Baker	Hope 1901, Walter Ewing
	22	Class of 1883	Luther, Mrs. Charles F.
	23	Clark 1864, George H. Clark 1874, Robert S.	McKenzie, Mrs. Charles T.
	24	Scheide, William Taylor	Caldwell Jr., Mrs. James H.
	25	McClintock 1872, Andrew H.	McClintock, Gilbert S.
	26	Sales Jr. 1926, Murray W.	Sales, Murray W.
	27	Reitzel Jr. 1927, Frank S.	Reitzel, Mr. and Mrs. Frank S.

	IN MEMORY OF	DONOR	LOCATION
28	Ballantyne, James Alexander	Ballantyne 1917, Howard P.	*Nave*
29	Imbrie, Charlotte Martha	Imbrie, Andrew C.	
30	Borden, Edward Shirley	Borden, Edward Shirley	
31	Roe, Rhuamy A.	Roe, Irving L.	
32	Carton, Frederic B.	Carton, L. A.	
33	Closson, James Harwood	Closson, Mary E. Bell Crowther, Mrs. Laurence Closson 3rd, James Harwood Closson, Mary Bancroft	
34	Azoy, Anastasio C. M.	Azoy, Mrs. A. C. M. Azoy 1914, A. C. M. Azoy 1920, Geoffrey V.	
35	Denegre 1889, James D.	Denegre, Mrs. James D.	
36	Peters, Ralph	Peters Jr., Ralph	
37	Milbank, Albert J.	Milbank, Albert G.	
38	Rolston, Mr. and Mrs. William	Rolston 1910, Brown	
39	Vanderpool Memorial Pew	Vanderpool, Wynant	
40	Wilson, Mary B.	Wilson, Walter O.	
41	Rieman, Annie Lowe	Rieman, Charles Rieman, Perlee Lowe	
42	Taylor 1895, Knox	Huntington 1895, Theodore S.	
43	Woods 1891, Lawrence C.	Woods, Mrs. Lawrence C. Woods, Mrs. Francis Woods Jr. 1922, Lawrence C.	
44	Cauldwell 1881, Thomas W.	Cauldwell, Charles M.	
45	Black 1845, Charles N.	Black 1893, James D.	
46	Cauldwell 1884, Samuel M.	Cauldwell, Charles M.	
47		Dennis 1879, Alfred Lewis	
48	Massey, Mina R.	Massey, William E. Massey, Jr. 1922, William E. Massey, R. B. R.	
49	Speir 1877, Francis	Pyne, Mrs. Moses Taylor	
50	Fiske 1918, Newell Rodney	Fiske, Harvey N.	
51	Wilkins 1897, Robert C.	Wilkins 1894, J. F.	
52	Mathey, Mrs. Josephine D.	Mathey 1912, Dean	
53	Annan 1885, John E.	Scribner, Mrs. Arthur H.	
54	Woodhull 1854, Addison W.	Woodhull, Daniel E.	
55	Rutherfurd 1776, John Rutherfurd 1806, Robert	Rutherfurd, Livingston Rutherfurd, Morris	

LOCATION		IN MEMORY OF	DONOR
Nave	56	Ely 1804, Alfred	Meade, Helena Rutherfurd Ely
			Ely 1905, Alfred
			Ely, Elizabeth Brewster
	57	Jessup 1886, Dr. and Mrs. W.	Jadwin, Stanley P.
	58	Halsey Jr. 1894, Edmund D.	Kellogg, Mrs. Frederick R.
	59	Brooks, Mary Ann	Brooks, John H.
	60	Halsey 1860, Edmund D.	Kellogg, Mrs. Frederick R.
	61	Farman, Samuel Ward	Farman, Miss Ida
	62	Williams 1881, Robert	Williams, Mrs. Robert
	63	Johnson, Frances E. H.	Johnson, Walter L.
	64	Gulick, Almira Reading	Gulick, Alexander R.
	65	Guy 1833, Alexander	Guy, William E.
		Guy 1860, Edward A.	
		Guy 1862, David W.	
		Guy 1865, William E.	
		Guy 1917, W. Edwin	
		Guy 1919, David Wade	
		Lemoine 1845, Edward S.	
	66	Gulick, Annie Rhodes	Gulick, Alexander R.
	67	Halsey 1898, Charles W.	Foster, Howard C.
	68	Davis, Julie Vietor	Davis 1900, J. Lionberger
	69	Keasbey 1869, Edward Quinton	Keasbey, Mrs. Edward Q.
	70	Davis, Marion Lionberger	Davis 1900, J. Lionberger
	71	Rouse, Elizabeth Hyatt	Rouse, John G.
		Rouse, William Chapman	
	72	Davis 1872, John David	Davis 1900, J. Lionberger
	73	Bulkley 1919, Harold Kidder	Bulkley, Edwin M.
	74	McPherson 1874, Simon John	McPherson 1906, John F.
			McPherson 1914, Paul C.
			McPherson 1906, O. H.
			Wright 1902, Raymond G.
			Raymond, Mrs. C. Harlow
	75	Handy, Parker	Handy 1879, Parker D.
	76	Todd 1876, Henry Alfred	Todd, Mrs. Henry A.
	77	Jacobus 1834, Melancthon W.	Jacobus Jr. 1877, M. W.
			Jacobus 3rd 1929, M. W.
	78	Coble 1898, Dwight H.	Coble, Mrs. Dwight H.
		Coble, Dwight S.	Coble, Mr. and Mrs. H. S.
	79	Halsey 1879, Abram Woodruff	Class of 1879
	80	Coursen, Jane Chester	Coursen 1881, William Abram
	81	Moore 1881, J. Leverett	Class of 1881

	IN MEMORY OF	DONOR	LOCATION
82	Baker 1913, Charles Dabney	Kennedy, Mrs. John S.	*Nave*
83	Parmly 1883, John Ehrick	Parmly, Mrs. John Ehrick	
84	Tod 1884, William Stewart	Kennedy, Mrs. John S.	
85	Wilson 1864, Moses Fleming	Fleming 1886, Mr. and Mrs. Matthew C.	
86	honoring: Fleming 1931, William W. Fleming Jr. 1921, Matthew C.	Fleming 1886, Matthew C.	
87	Rollins, Edward Ashton	Rollins, Philip A.	
88		Class of 1888	
89	Spring 1766, Alpheus	Rollins, Philip A.	
90	Furst, Austin O.	Furst, William S.	
91	Payne, Calvin Nathaniel	Payne 1895, Christy Payne 1891, Francis H.	
92	Hodge, Elsie Sinclair	D'Olier, Franklin	
93	Hodge 1893, Cortlandt Van R.	D'Olier, Franklin	
94		Class of 1894	
95		Class of 1895	
96		Class of 1896	
97		Class of 1897	
98	Woods 1892, Richard Flavel	Hart 1892, Charles D. Riggs 1892, Alfred R.	
99	Class of 1899	Fuller, Mortimer B.	
100	Class of 1900	King, Frederick P.	
101	Gosnell, Mary Denmead Gosnell, Frank	Gosnell, H. A.	
102	Dickson 1900, James Reid	Lathrop, Henry R.	
103	Bonsall 1902, James Malcolm	Bonsall, Mrs. James Malcolm	
104	Laidlaw 1904, Robert Remsen	Laidlaw, Mrs. Robert R.	
105	Chandlee Jr. 1905, Evan G.	Chandlee, Charles W. Chandlee, Edward E.	
106	Howe 1891, Edward Leavitt	Howe, Mrs. Edward Leavitt	
107	Greene, Arthur M. Greene, Eleanor J. Lewis, Jean Alexander Lewis, T. A.	Greene Jr., Dean and Mrs. Arthur M.	
108	Brown 1887, Stewart	Brown, Mrs. Stewart	
109	Grandin Jr. 1894, William James	Grandin, Frank S.	
110	Rockwood Jr., Charles G.	Rockwood, Miss Katherine	
111	McKelvy, Louise Wood	McKelvy, Robert	

LOCATION		IN MEMORY OF	DONOR
Nave	112	Duffield 1876, John Fletcher	Duffield 1892, Edward Dickinson
	113	Patterson Jr. 1913, Robert W.	Class of 1913, Section of Cottage Club
	114	Shields Jr. 1891, George Howell Shields III 1931, George Howell	Shields, Mrs. George H.
	115	Duffield, Mrs. John Thomas	Duffield, Edward D.
	116	Osborn, Gurdon S.	Osborn 1877, Mr. and Mrs. Henry Fairfield
	117	Thompson 1877, Henry Burling	Thompson Jr. 1920, Henry Burling Thompson 1928, James Harrison Wilson
	118	Beekman 1918, Leonard	Beekman, Edgar
	119	George 1908, Louis B.	Bangs, William D.
	120	Sherrill, Andrew M. Sherrill 1909, Howard W.	Sherrill, Mrs. Andrew M.
		Kimball 1904, Walter Denniston (*unnumbered pew*)	Kimball, Mildred B. Kimball, W. Brice Kimball 1940, Peter D.
		Kimball 1904, Walter D. (*unnumbered pew*)	Kimball, Mrs. Walter D.
		Rogers 1904, Lawrence H. (*unnumbered pew*)	Rogers 1947, Fred B.
	131	Parmly 1879, Eleazar	Parmly, George
	132	Peirce 1909, Caleb C.	Taylor, Mrs. Ruth Peirce
	133	Gardner, Frederick Dozier	Gardner 1924, Dozier Lee
	134	Dibble 1927, Huntley D.	Dibble, Mr. and Mrs. Samuel F.
	135	Tomlinson, Ernest H.	Tomlinson, Mrs. Ernest H. Tomlinson 1916, Norman B.
	136	Waring 1891, Orville G.	Waring, Mrs. Orville G.
	137	Milbank, Georgianna G.	Milbank, Albert G.
	138	Mitchell 1861, Samuel S.	Mitchell, James McC.
	139	Cauldwell, Charles Milbank	Cauldwell, Miss Sophia L.
	147	Clarkson 1952, Peter S.	Clarkson, Mr. and Mrs. Robert L.
	148	Stewart 1897, William A. W.	Stewart, Mrs. William A. W.
	149	Kokot, Irene	Rogozinski, Z. R.
	150	McLanahan 1873, Samuel	His Sons
	155	Ballard 1929, Horatio Biglow	Ballard, Edward L.
	167	Johnson 1867, William M.	Johnson, William K. Johnson, George W.
	170	Perkins 1872, Joseph F.	Kilpatrick, John D.

IN MEMORY OF	DONOR	LOCATION
180 Coursen, Mrs. Elizabeth R.	Coursen 1881, William A.	*Nave*
201 Cochran 1896, James B.	Cochran 1900, Henry J.	
202 Hancock Jr., James	Hancock 1888, James	
A* Pierson, Carrie Booth N.	Pierson, Samuel Pierson 1914, Richard N. Pierson, Samuel N. Pierson 1911, Norris E.	*Braman Transept*
B Smith, Sue L. B. Smith, A. Alexander	Smith 1901, H. Alexander Smith, W. Schuyler	
C Godfrey, Sophie A.	Godfrey 1896, Aaron W.	
D Davis, Amy Chirm Davis, Elisha Thomas	Davis, Courtenay C.	
E Burns, Helen Rouse	Burns, J. Rouse	
F Langenberg, Henry Frederick	Langenberg 1900, Harry Hill	
G Carter 1899, Norman McL.	Carter, Samuel T. Carter, Howard Carter, Robert Carter, Reginald L. Carter Jr., Samuel T. Cook, Mrs. O. F. Carter, G. Herbert Schultz, Mrs. William M. Clarke, Mrs. Roger H. Bayliss, Mrs. Roswell S.	
H English 1865, Nicholas C. J.	English 1899, Conover	
I Wheeler, Arthur Dana	Wheeler, Mrs. Anna H. Wheeler, Gordon B.	
J Currier, Jennie Ritchie	Currier, Harry G. Currier Jr. 1916, Harry G. Currier 1913, John R.	
K Riggs 1885, William P.	Riggs 1883, Lawrason	
L Riggs 1897, Thomas Dudley	Riggs, Jesse B. Riggs 1892, Alfred R. Riggs 1894, Henry G. Riggs 1894, Francis G.	

* In the east half of this pew is the accustomed seat of the wife of President Emeritus Harold W. Dodds. Her name and two lines from the chorus of a favorite hymn commemorate this fact. The inscription is the gift of H. P. Van Dusen, Class of 1919.

Margaret Murray Dodds
"Lord, Thy glory fills the heaven,
Earth is with thy fullness stored."

The need to increase the size of the sanctuary in the apsidal chapel of Marquand Transept has led to some reorganization of the seating. The changes are indicated by brackets after Pews MM, O, and U.

LOCATION		IN MEMORY OF	DONOR
Marquand Transept	M*	Brady 1895, Henry Hervey Brady 1924, Clarence S.	Brady, Mrs. Henry Hervey
	M*	Jones, Virginia B.	Jones, E. Lester
		[*Moved to follow Pew T]	
	N	Drummond Jr. 1936, John H.	Drummond 1922, Kenneth
	N	Drummond, Thomas J.	Drummond, Margaret H. Drummond 1910, John Drummond 1914, Douglas Drummond 1922, Kenneth
	O*	Dickson 1900, James Reid	Lathrop, Henry R.
		[*Moved to the Chapel Choir Crypt]	
	P	Burrage 1913, Percy Fraser	Burrage, Mrs. Robert L.
	Q	Van Dusen 1915, Edwin Thorp	Thorp, Mrs. W. Edwin
	R	Hepburn 1803, Samuel Patton 1863, John Woodbridge Hepburn 1823, James Curtis	Patton 1899, Henry B.
	S	Frame 1897, John Musser	Frame, Mrs. Lizzie A.
	T	Parker 1899, Clarence H. Parker 1898, John Reid	Parker, Mrs. Lydia Parker, Charles H.
	U*		
		[*Moved to the Chapel Choir Crypt]	
	V	Rankin, William Rankin, Ellen Hope	Bliss, Ellen Rankin Rankin, Walter M.
	W	Reynolds 1897, Theodore F.	Reynolds, Mrs. Theodore F.
	X	Wood, J. Harry	Wood 1903, Charles M.
Gallery	G-1	Simpson 1833, Josiah Simpson 1794, John	McCutcheon 1915, Brunson S.
	G-2	Hamill 1880, Samuel	Prentice, Mrs. William Kelly
	G-3	MacGregor 1888, Robert W.	MacGregor, Mrs. Robert W.
	G-4	McWilliams 1892, Clarence McWilliams, Mr. and Mrs. Daniel W.	Miss McWilliams Howard McWilliams
	G-5	DeMund 1823, Isaac S.	Hegeman, Mrs. Daniel V.
	G-6	Urquhart 1927, Richard	Urquhart, Mrs. Richard A.

IN MEMORY OF	DONOR	LOCATION
G-7 Smith, Henry A. Weed, James B.	Smith 1896, Ralph D.	*Gallery*
G-8 McVitty, Phoebe Q.	McVitty, Samuel H.	
G-9 Danenhower, John C.	Danenhower, Mrs. Alice	
G-10 Class of 1890	Moles, E. J.	
G-11 Dillon, Mr. and Mrs. David M.	Dillon 1907, Herbert Lowell	
G-12 Claggett 1764, Thomas John	Williams, George W.	
G-13 Bannerman VI, Frank	Bannerman, David B.	
G-14 Bronson, Clara E. S.	Bronson, Adelbert E.	
G-15 Brown, William Henry	Brown, Frank	
G-18 Hussey Jr. 1922, John U.	Hussey, John U.	

G-20 IN HONOR OF:
      Drummond 1910, John H.
      Merle-Smith 1911, V. S.
      Osborn 1883, William Church
	Princeton Fund Committee	

STONE SEATS

Note: The bays are numbered from west to east, beginning after one has entered from the narthex.

1st bay Jamison 1891, Charles M.	Jamison, Cecelia Rayburn Jamison, Jr., Charles M. Jamison, James Rayburn Jamison, Janet Martin	*Nave: North Aisle*
2nd bay Vance, James Nelson Vance, Lillie McClellan	Vance 1886, Henry Edgerton Vance Jr., James Nelson Vance 1901, William McClellan	

3rd bay McGill Jr. 1858, George McC.
        McGill 1864, Alexander T.
        Gamble, Mary McGill
        McGill 1867, John Dale
        McGill 1877, Samuel Hepburn
	Lane, Mrs. Charles S.	

4th bay Shellabarger 1909, Samuel	Shellabarger, Mrs. Samuel	
4th bay Studdiford 1888, William E.	Palmer, Mrs. Edgar	
1st bay Davie 1776, William R.	Davie 1868, George M.	*Nave: South Aisle*
2nd bay Stockton Jr. 1851, Robert F.	Pyne, Mrs. Moses Taylor	
3rd bay Stockton 1820, Robert F.	Pyne, Mrs. Moses Taylor	
4th bay Stockton 1748, Richard (Signer)	Pyne, Mrs. Moses Taylor	
5th bay Sherrerd, Thomas	Sherrerd, William D.	

21 North Aisle

IN MEMORY OF	DONOR	LOCATION
Bonner, 1896	Bonner 1914, Kenneth	*Braman Transept,*
Fordyce, Alexander Robert	Fordyce 1896, Alexander R. Jr.	*in Wall Arcade*
Sturges, Frederick		
Lane 1892, Charles Seth	Lane 1900, John McGill	
Sheldon 1875, Thomas		
Wiggin 1880, Alfred		
Church 1891, Theodore Winthrop		*Marquand Transept,*
Burr 1895, James Edward		*in Wall Arcade*
Elsworth 1911, Edward J.		
The Class of 1873		

INSCRIPTIONS

Memorials in the form of inscriptions signify contributions to the Chapel Endowment Fund if names of donors are included.

Wall Stones

1st bay Imbrie 1900, Harold	LeBoutillier 1900, Philip	*Nave: North Aisle*
1st bay Vail 1902, Charles Edward	Class of 1902	Plate 21
1st bay Tower 1894, William H.	Tower, Florence Curran	
2nd bay Angas, W. Mack	Angas, Mrs. W. Mack	
2nd bay Bachman Jr. 1899 Robert	Staake 1899, William W.	
2nd bay Staake 1899, William W.	Staake, Mrs. Lois McCall	
2nd bay Robbins 1889, Edmund Yard		
2nd bay Bedford 1897, Paul		
3rd bay Lyman 1918, Alexander V.	Lyman, Miss Frances	
3rd bay Iams 1901, Samuel Harvey		
3rd bay Buchanan, Charity Packer	Buchanan 1909, John Grier	
Buchanan Jr. 1938, John Grier	Buchanan Jr., Mrs. John G.	
3rd bay Tasker 1927, Frank Griswold	Tasley, Mildred L.	
4th bay McClure 1888, Charles F. W.	McClure, Grace L. J.	
Opp.		
col. 5 Mathey, Gertrude Winans	Mathey 1912, Dean	
3rd bay Creasey, Edward James		*Nave: South Aisle*
Creasey, M. Anna B. H.		
Hendrickson, Emeline B.		
Hendrickson, John L.		

LOCATION	IN MEMORY OF	DONOR
Nave: South Aisle	4th bay Witherspoon, John	
	4th bay Duffield 1892, Edward D.	Yeatman, Mrs. Philip W.
	4th bay Rush 1760, Benjamin	
	4th bay Rush 1797, Richard	
	1st bay Kleinhans 1900, Mr. and Mrs. Lewis C.	Their Sons
	Opp. col. 5 Dell 1912, Burnham North	
	5th bay Wintringer 1894, George C.	
Marquand Transept	Marquand, Henry G.	
	McCosh, James	
	Murray, James Ormsbee	
	Guyot, Arnold	
	Henry, Joseph	
	Seeley, George Perry	Seeley Jr. 1900, G. P.
		Seeley 1911, DeB. K.
	Shepard 1929, Francis Guernsey	
	Loomis, Elmer Howard	
Braman Transept	Gulick 1892, Archibald	
	Parrott 1888, Thomas Marc	
	Cardona Fox, Hanna	

Plaques

Braman Transept	Bovaird 1889, David Miner	Class of 1889
	Rogers 1903, David Miner	Class of 1903
	Church 1888, James Robb	Church 1892, Alonzo
Marquand Transept	Hodge 1893, Cortlandt Van R.	
	Taylor 1882, George Yardley	

Bronze Relief

Marquand Transept	McCosh, James	Class of 1879

Columns

North Aisle	1st bay Watres 1901, Harold Arthur	Watres, Louis A.
	2nd bay Jones 1887, Mr. and Mrs. W. L.	Jones Jr. 1915, William L.

IN MEMORY OF	DONOR	LOCATION
4th bay McCarter 1842, Thomas Nesbitt	McCarter 1882, Uzal H. McCarter 1888, Thomas N. McCarter 1879, Robert H.	*North Aisle*
2nd bay Munger 1892, Max	Munger 1884, Henry C.	*South Aisle*
3rd bay Hunter 1772, Andrew	Landon 1881, Francis G. Pratt, Mary Landon	

LANTERNS

2nd bay "Given in Thanksgiving"	Cox, Miss Susan Alfreda	*North Side*
4th bay Shellabarger 1947, John Eric	Shellabarger, Mr. and Mrs. Samuel	
2nd bay Lambert Jr., Gerald Barnes	Clopton, Mrs. Malvern	*South Side*
4th bay Aldrich, William Learned	Aldrich, Dean and Mrs. Donald	
	Mathey 1912, Dean	*Crossing, North Side*
	Gulick 1897, Archibald	*Crossing, South Side*
	Poe III, Mrs. John	*Passage to Dean's Study*

PANELING

The oak paneling was presented by William Caldwell Roberts, Class of 1930, in memory of his father, William Henry Roberts, Class of 1895. On the left is a medallion with the figure of a man led by a "seeing eye" dog. Around it is an inscription in Welsh: Lle yr oeddwn I yn ddall yr wyf fi yn awr yn gweled—"[one thing I know] that whereas I was blind, now I see." (John 9:25) The reference is to Mr. W. H. Roberts' work in behalf of the blind. Balancing this medallion is one with the arms of MacLean, referring to Mr. Roberts' Scottish heritage.   *Apsidal Chapel*

When the paneling was installed, the wall inscription recording that the two windows above are a memorial to Cornelius C. Cuyler given by his daughter Eleanor De Graff Cuyler, was covered over. The dedication is now recorded on a tablet affixed to the paneling.

The carved panel in the crypt is in memory of Alfred James McClure, 1906   *Crypt*

ORGANS

The main organ was given by Helena Woolworth McCann in memory of Frank Winfield Woolworth.

The echo organ in the gallery was given in memory of Albert Frost Earnshaw, Class of 1892, by Archibald A. Gulick, Class of 1897.

FURNISHINGS

Nave

Pulpit

The Pulpit was given in memory of Wilton Merle-Smith, Class of 1877, by Mrs. Wilton Merle-Smith and the Class of 1877. The Pulpit Fall was given by Carl D. Reimers.

Lectern

The Lectern was given in memory of Robert Cooper, Class of 1763, by John Grier Hibben. The Lectern Markers were given by Carl D. Reimers.

Flags

The Church Flag at the pulpit was given by H. Pitney Van Dusen, Class of 1919. The Processional Flag was given in memory of Nathan Southwick Schroeder, Class of 1898, by the Class of 1898. The National Flag at the crossing was given in memory of Arthur Richmond Taber, Class of 1917 by Sydney R. Taber, Class of 1883.

Alms Basons

The Alms Basons were given by Archibald A. Gulick, Class of 1897.

Marquand Transept

The furnishings of the Apsidal Chapel are the gift of the Right Reverend Paul Matthew, Class of 1887, with the exception of the following:

	IN MEMORY OF	DONOR
Font		Frelinghusen 1931, Major Theodore, *Donor Vitae* 1943
Book of Common Prayer on Lectern		Martha Mildred Smith
Bible on Communion Table		Samuel Dodds
Candlesticks on Altar	Dean Aldrich	Mrs. Clopton

The Cross

Choir

The Cross behind the Holy Table is in memory of Moses Taylor Pyne, Jr., Class of 1908. It was given by his daughter, Miss Agnes L. Pyne.

Stand for the Cross

The stand was given in memory of Peter Bent Northrup Wallis, Class of 1957, by his parents, Everett S. Wallis and Mary Northrup Wallis.

The Holy Table

The illumination of the carved panels on the front of the table is recorded in an inscription on its north end.

To the Glory of God
in memory of
George Black Stewart 1896
Trustee 1887-1932

Given by the members of
his family

The Vases

The vases on the Holy Table are in memory of Allan Marquand, Class of 1874. *Choir*
Given by Mrs. Allan Marquand. Two additional vases are in memory of Albridge
Clinton Smith, Class of 1903. Given by Mrs. Albridge C. Smith.

The Coverlet

The original coverlet for the Holy Table was in memory of Arthur V. Savage,
Class of 1917, given by his mother, Mrs. Charles C. Savage. The new coverlet is
in memory of Charles Chauncey Savage, Class of 1873, Anne Vandervoort Savage,
and Arthur Vandervoort Savage, Class of 1917, given by their children.

The Communion Service

The silver service used at the Sacrament of the Lord's Supper was the graduation
gift of the Class of 1884 and was used in the original Marquand Chapel. Another
set is the gift of Charles G. Rockwood.

The Chalices

Two of the chalices are in memory of Alexander Howard Nelson, Class of 1895,
and Alexander Kirkpatrick Nelson, Class of 1927. Given by Eliza McCandless
Nelson. Two are in memory of Lewis Ferry Moody and Eleanor Greene Moody.
Given by Lewis Ferry Moody, Jr., Class of 1932, Arthur M. G. Moody, Class of
1933, and Eleanor Moody Broadhurst.

The Patens

One of the patens is the gift of Milton Darlington Moore, Class of 1919, and
Russell McPherson Moore, Class of 1946. One is given in memory of George
Louis Russell, Jr., by Dorothy Christ Russell and George Louis Russell, III, Class
of 1940. One is given in memory of Grady Lee Smith, Class of 1953, by his friends
and classmates.

The Altar Cloth

A hand-woven linen altar cloth from the Island of Cyprus is the gift of Gertrude
Winans Mathey.

The Holy Communion Service Books

One of the Service Books used in the Holy Communion is in memory of Frank
Henry Constant. Given by Annette Woodbridge Constant. The other Service
Book is given in memory of Mary Elizabeth Lewis Greene and Arthur Maurice
Greene, Jr. The Service Book of Holy Communion (Episcopal usage) is given in
memory of Martha Mildred Smith by Richard Smith.

The Bibles

The Bible on the Holy Table was given in memory of Hildegarde Berkmans by
Bruce Berkmans, Class of 1922, and Bruce Berkmans, Jr., Class of 1952. The

Bible on the Lectern is the gift of Carl H. Pforzheimer. The Bibles on the Prayer Desks were given in memory of Kenneth C. Harris, Class of 1965, by Major and Mrs. Kenneth Watts.

The Lectern Desk

The Lectern Desk is in memory of Richard Hansford Burroughs, Jr., Class of 1939. Given by his parents, Mr. and Mrs. R. H. Burroughs.

Lectern

The small Lectern was given in memory of John Prentiss Poe, III, Class of 1922, by Lydia Taber Poe.

The Prayer Desks

The Prayer Desks are in memory of Kenneth C. Harris, Class of 1965, given by Tiger Inn, and of Raymond Denkmann Reimers, Class of 1905, given by his family.

Anonymous Gifts

These include a silver baptismal bowl, two portal boards, communion linen, the Sacristy furnishings, the rug before the Holy Table.

The Cushions

The Cushions in the first bay of the south side of the choir were designed for the persons who normally occupied assigned places at the time the cushions were made. Janet Frantz Cottier executed the designs of William Feay Shellman, Jr.

Robert Francis Goheen, President: In the center, the arms of Princeton University. Above, the initials R. F. G.; below, date 1964. The surrounding shields are: Athena's Owl, for Classical Studies; Republic of India (place of birth); Lawrenceville School; 1st Cavalry Division insignia (World War II service).

Ernest Gordon, The Dean of the Chapel: In the center, the badge of Scotland, the Thistle. Above, initials E. G.; below, date 1964. The surrounding shields are: Princess Louise's Own Regiment; Rampant Lion of Scotland; Gordon coat of arms; Princeton coat of arms. All superimposed on the Cross of Saint Andrew.

The Visiting Preacher: In the center a ship, representing the Church with sails decorated by crosses and an Anchor of Hope. Date 1969. All surrounded by the symbols of the four Evangelists, two of which hold the Princeton arms.

J. Merrill Knapp, Dean: In center initials J. M. K. and U. S. naval insignia with date 1965, flanked by the arms of Princeton and Yale supported by a Tiger and a Yale. Two small devices suggest musical interests—at upper left, a horn and harp, at upper right, a "whiffenpoof."

William D'O. Lippincott, Dean: Three shields at center, one with initials W. D'O. L.; the arms of Princeton supported by the Griffin of St. George's School, Newport; the arms of St. George's School and the Princeton Tiger. At the edges of the cushion are six badges reflecting various interests.

The cassapanca is the gift of Davenport West, Class of 1905. The tapestry is the gift of David L. Frothingham, Class of 1943.

"The Man of Sorrows," bronze, was presented to the Chapel by the sculptor, Helen D. Goldberg.

The Memorial Cabinet was given by Archibald A. Gulick, Class of 1897, and his classmates.

EXTERIOR

THE BRIGHT PULPIT

Built into the angle of the south transept and the nave is the Bright Pulpit. On the west face is the inscription:

IN MEMORIAM
JOHN BRIGHT
1811–1889
THE GREAT BRITISH
COMMONER AND
FRIEND OF AMERICA
IN HER TIME OF NEED
FLORENCE BROOKS-ATEN

The south face of the pulpit bears the quotation from Bright:

AN INSTRUCTED DEMOCRACY
IS THE SUREST FOUNDATION
OF GOVERNMENT AND
EDUCATION AND
FREEDOM ARE THE
ONLY SOURCES OF
TRUE GREATNESS AND
HAPPINESS AMONG
ANY PEOPLE

THE HIBBEN GARDEN

Close against the north transept of the Chapel is a small formal garden with a bench on which is inscribed:

COME YE YOURSELVES APART
INTO A LONELY PLACE
AND REST AWHILE

The garden is designated by an inscription on the eastern buttress of the transept:

IN MEMORY OF
DR. JOHN GRIER HIBBEN
CLASS OF 1882
MINISTER OF THE GOSPEL
TEACHER OF MEN
PRESIDENT OF PRINCETON
UNIVERSITY, 1912 TO 1932
UNDER WHOSE ADMINISTRATION
THIS CHAPEL WAS BUILT

INDEX

*This index lists the donors of memorial gifts to the Chapel
and the persons whom the gifts commemorate.*